EVERGREEN
AFFILIATE
MARKETING

EVERGREEN
AFFILIATE
MARKETING

*Master the Mindset, Learn the Strategies
and Apply the Systems Used by the
World's Wealthiest Affiliate Marketers*

By Nathaniel McCallister

Contents

Acknowledgements

This book and my career as an internet entrepreneur wouldn't be possible without the love and support of my beautiful wife, Emily. Your endless support and unconditional love have been more important to my life than you may ever know. I love you.

As for the contents of this book, oh how I wish I could take credit for every idea, concept, and tactic I'm going to share with you. However, if I filled these pages only with my original ideas, it would look more like a pamphlet than a book. Only a fraction of the things that I know are unique to me. Even the things that I might believe are ideas I discovered were likely a result of passive exposure to someone smarter than myself. It's more likely that I simply don't recall when or where I was introduced to any concept that seems original than it being truly original.

Everything I've done results from the people who have gone before me. Whether they intentionally shared their knowledge with me or did so indirectly, most of what I know resulted from osmosis rather than divine enlightenment.

So I want to take a minute and give credit and acknowledgement to the many people who have either directly or indirectly improved knowledge of internet marketing and, as a result, my entire life. In alphabetical order they are: David Allen, James Altucher, Chris Anderson, Jay Baer, Jacob Bates, Robert W. Bly, Skye Brant, Les Brown, Russell Brunson, Brian Burt, Dale Carnegie, Robert B. Cialdini, PhD, James Clear, Eric Cyprus, Ray Dalio, Kim Dang, Ryan Deiss, Barbara Drazga, Chris Ducker, John Lee Dumas, Ray Edwards, Hal Elrod, Nir Eyal, Tim Ferriss, Michael Flanagan, Pat Flynn, Chris Fong, Scott Fox, Jason Fried, Dylan Frost, Mike Garner, Connor Gillivan, Malcom Gladwell, Seth Godin, Christopher Grant, Chris Green, Chris Guillebeau, Daren Hardy, Jason Harris, Spencer Haws, Nathan Hirsch, Ryan Holiday, Peter Hollins, Chet Holmes, Michael Hyatt, Liam James Kay, Gary Keller, Frank Kern, W. Chan Kim, Robert Kiyosaki, Austin Kleon, Eric Lambert, Jessica Larrew, John Lawson, Ryan Levesque, Eddie Levine, Mark Manson, Perry Marshall, Michael Matthews, Tucker Max, David McRaney, Daniel Meadors, Spencer Mecham, Rachel Miller, Jon Morrow, Alex Moss, Cal Newport, David Ogilvy, Neil Patel, Molly Pittman, Ian Pribyl, Joe Pulizzi, Steve Raiken, Robbie Richards, Travis Ross, Nathan Ruff, Javier San Juan, Arnold Schwarzennegger, Ramit Sethi, Amy Shmittauer, Eric Siu, Chris Smith, Stephen Smotherman, Bob Steele, Michael Stelzner, Cynthia Stine, Brenden Sullivan, Dan Sullivan, Ken Szovati, Steve Teneriello, Gary Vaynerchuk, Jeff Walker, Drew Eric Whitman, Chris Wilkey, Paul Witter, Matthew Woodward, and Zig Ziglar. You've all helped me whether you realized it or not, and for that I am truly grateful.

I also want to thank everyone who has followed me and supported me in my journey, regardless of whether you've purchased anything from me or any of the brands I endorse.

Foreword

You're likely one of two kinds of people if you've picked up this book. You've either already started making money with affiliate marketing and want to continue to grow that income, or you're ready to try affiliate marketing for the first time.

It doesn't matter which person you are. You've made it to the right place, and I'll explain why you will want to study and implement the strategies and systems in this book. But first, some backstory.

Despite growing up just a block or two from each other in the suburbs of Columbus, Ohio, I didn't "meet" Nate until I was about thirty years old. I was trying to take my own e-commerce business to the next level, and Nate runs one of the largest Amazon seller Facebook groups that there is.

I also wanted more. I had dabbled in affiliate marketing in the past without any success, posting links to places like Craigslist when it was still a "legitimate" method of getting customers.

I was able to see what Nate was doing in his own affiliate business, and it made me want to learn more. How to market properly, grow an audience, be able to refer that audience to high caliber and useful products. You see, I knew in my bones that was the right thing to do. Spamming links, black hat SEO, and the lot will only get you so far. You need to do things the right way, and you need to do it for two reasons.

1. You want to be able to sleep at night and not feel like a slimy marketer.
2. You need to grow a real business. Not something that will disappear in the next social media or SEO slap.

So I reached out to Nate. Took a page out of his own playbook and offered something of value—a small piece of software I had built based on a post he made.

Out of that was born something really great. A teacher I could learn new things from, a partner on several affiliate launches, and even software products to the tune of over $900,000 in revenue, and most importantly a friend.

Now why should you spend some of the 168 hours (less after you factor in job, family, and responsibilities) you have in a week studying the material in this book? Plainly, it works. It doesn't just work last year or right now. These are systems and strategies that you can implement now and into the future. You will be able to start, build, and grow a sustainable business from the comfort of your office chair.

A Warning! Before you go on, you should know what this book is not. It is not a get-rich-quick book. You will not become a millionaire in the next thirty days. You also won't be living life on easy street collecting checks from passive income.

Affiliate marketing requires strategies like audience building, content creation, and more, which will take time and effort. You will need to act on what you learn from the pages of this book and eventually, over time you will see that you have built a nice income for yourself. What Nate likes to call "pastive" income for the work and sweat equity you've put in in the past that will pay dividends into the future.

Before we wrap up, I'd like to add to the instructions already included in this book.

Don't just read this and put it up on the shelf. Study the contents, make notes, highlight important parts, and even dog-ear some pages. Take action and implement what you learn. Today, not tomorrow or next week. You will be best served to try something out while it's fresh in your mind and you will cement the learning process that way.

Don't be afraid to fail. Trying something new, especially with skin in the game like your time or even money, will often lead to greater successes down the road. Perhaps Mark Cuban says it best:

 "It doesn't matter how many times you fail. It doesn't matter how many times you almost get it right. No one is going to know or care about your failures, and neither should you. All you have to do is learn from them and those around you because . . . all that matters in business is that you get it right once. Then everyone can tell you how lucky you are."

Now grab your pencil and your highlighter, and go learn some strategies to implement in your own affiliate business.

I look forward to hearing about the success stories that come from the readers of this book. I even look forward to, hopefully, buying a product, a course, or a software program using one of your affiliate links in the future.

I hope you enjoy this book as thoroughly as I enjoyed being able to write this short foreword. I believe in the positive power of affiliate marketing and the concepts in this book, and I know that if you cultivate the skills and implement them, you will come out the other side a happier and more prosperous reader.

Good luck and good reading!

—Christopher Grant

INTRODUCTION

Before Our Journey

If you're like me, you're probably champing at the bit to get into the meat of this book. You're ready to learn the things that will help you build a thriving affiliate marketing business. However, before I get into the real nuts and bolts, we need to cover some caveats. I promise to keep this brief, but please do read this chapter before continuing. It may save you a good bit of time and money.

First, I want to thank and congratulate you for taking the leap of faith to read *Evergreen Affiliate Marketing*. Your time is your most precious resource, and I'm humbled that you're willing to trust me with several of your finite hours of life. I don't take that responsibility lightly, and I believe that your time spent in reading the pages that follow deserves a massive ROI (return on investment). I've written this book with that in mind. If you give me this investment of your time and focus, I promise I will make you a better affiliate marketer permanently.

In a world that associates price with value, this book is an exception to the rule. The content in this book far outweighs the cost you've paid. If after reading *Evergreen Affiliate Marketing* you don't feel it has provided exponentially more value than it cost in both money and time, I encourage you to get a full refund. I am confident you will find tremendous value, but if for any reason you don't, I do not want your money.

If after reading *Evergreen Affiliate Marketing* you don't feel it has provided exponentially more value than it cost in both money and time, I encourage you to get a full refund.

Also, I would appreciate it if you would also email me with any feedback (my contact information is at the end of the book). Although this book is far more affordable than the high ticket coaching programs and courses on the topic of affiliate marketing, it is as dense with insights as anything you will find on the market at any price point.

As much as I dislike this part, it's only fair and customary that I tell you about myself. My real name is Nate McCallister (I don't have any secret aliases like many writers in my space), and I've been in the affiliate marketing space since 2012. As cheesy as it sounds, money isn't how I measure my business success. I do, however, appreciate that it's a decent litmus test for someone who is trying to quickly vet my qualifications. Although it's a relative statement, in my career with affiliate marketing I've had the good fortune of earning what most people would consider a good amount of money. I am a top affiliate for several well-known, highly competitive programs and products. I've profited (net, after all costs) over $1,000,000 from one website alone but have income streams in multiple niches.

You should always take this sort of earnings statement with a grain of salt. How much I've earned doesn't necessarily mean that I'm a great fit to teach you how to do the same. I've seen countless wealthy affiliates who found outstanding success but aren't skilled with the ability to share how they did it in a way that is easy to follow. Likewise, there are many "one-hit wonders" whose life-time earnings are not a reflection of their true skill set or their ability to repeat it if they had to start from scratch. This is where I am different.

I can start from scratch and create new affiliate income streams in any niche. I'm confident that if given just 30 days, I can easily create an additional source of affiliate income of at least $1,000/month in any niche without leveraging my existing assets. Not only do I know how to do this, I know how to explain my processes in ways that are easy for anyone to follow. This means you can more easily emulate my success.

Would you take advice on how to dunk a basketball from someone who is seven feet tall? This is what it's like if you're taking affiliate marketing advice from people who have massive audiences and have focused only on one niche for their entire careers. You need real-world, relatable advice, and I will give you exactly that.

Another way I am different from many of my peers is that affiliate marketing isn't the only facet of my internet business. I have various other ventures that are unrelated to affiliate marketing. Thanks to affiliate marketing, I'm able to sustain or grow my earnings while still having time to pursue my other projects.

Also, I don't make my living by teaching affiliate marketing. I make most of my income from applying the affiliate marketing skills I teach in this book across various niches and products. I wrote this book as a complete package of all the affiliate marketing knowledge I've gained over the years and know will work for many years to come. There is no "next product" for you to buy. Everything I want to share has been condensed into this book. Nothing has been held back.

While there are others who make more money than I do, my experience and perspective are uniquely valuable to my readers thanks to the broad scope of how I approach things. In contrast to the standard business advice to focus on one thing (which is usually excellent advice), I've adopted an "omni" approach to my affiliate marketing business. Instead of a singular focus, I test many strategies and mediums. Blogging, paid ads, video marketing, you name it and I've given it the old college try. Anything I mention in this book is from my real-world experiences and seeing what does and doesn't work at scale.

Besides my experience promoting products as an affiliate marketer, I've also been on the other side of affiliate marketing as an affiliate marketing manager for my own offers and products and those of many other businesses. This has given me a "big picture" view of what great affiliate marketing actually looks like, and this book will showcase that.

Okay, enough about me. Let me explain what is and isn't in this book.

What Is and Isn't in This Book

Let's start by setting your expectations for what this book is and what it is not. If this isn't exactly what you're looking for, I want you to discover that right away so you don't waste time and energy.

- ✔ Strategies and Principles That Last
- ✖ Gimmicks and Black Hat Tactics
- ✖ Filler Content that Wastes your Time
- ✖ Sales Pitch to a Course or Coaching

1. Evergreen Affiliate Marketing *Will Teach You Only the Strategies That Will Last the Test of Time*

evergreen adjective

🔖 Save Word

ev·er·green | \ ˈe-vər-ˌgrēn 🔊 \

Definition of *evergreen* (Entry 1 of 2)

1   : having foliage that remains green and functional through more than one growing season
    — compare DECIDUOUS sense 1

2   a   : retaining freshness or interest : PERENNIAL

      b   : universally and continually relevant : not limited in applicability to a particular event or date

I've read almost every book on affiliate marketing, and there weren't other books I felt would be relevant ten years from now. I wanted to write something that will last and will read just as well in print in 2021 when it was first published as it will in 2041 and beyond.

Yes, I could show you tips that are working at the time of this writing. Things that could increase the chances of a novice making $1,000/month quickly using TikTok. (If you're reading this in the future, that may sound wildly outdated and TikTok may very well no longer exist). I'm not opposed to this sort of content. I spend most of my time writing that sort of thing, but I save it for my blog, EntreResource.com.

I believe blogs should be timely but most books should be timeless. I can't come to your house years from now and take your copy of this book and scratch out the tactics that no longer work, and I don't want to ask you to buy countless revisions in the future.

My fear is that a printed copy of this book could eventually contain misleading tactics that no longer work. Tactics that could cause you to waste money and time (again, emphasis on time; this is a common theme in this book). Nothing kills the potential of an aspiring affiliate marketer quite like experts confidently showing them ways to lose money.

Almost all quick hacks and tips become played out by the time you hear about them unless you're extremely good at finding them early. I'm giving you the principles that will help you make consistent sales forever.

These principles will work regardless of the current climate at the time you're reading it. Regardless of what is trending, which social media channels are popular, or what new regulations are in place.

You'll notice that I've avoided mentioning social media platforms or search engines by name with rare exceptions. Most of the time, I'll be using phrases like "social media channels" instead of "Instagram." However, you will see references to Google and YouTube because I believe they are both here to stay.

This was painful. I know how great it is to find timely and specific things that can generate quick results. It was difficult to resist the urge to include many of the things that are working in 2021 as I'm writing. However, I know it's in the best interest of future readers and won't dampen the impact of the content. The underlying concepts remain the same, regardless of the name of the platform or how the interface looks.

I am also making exceptions regarding email marketing and search engine optimization. Both are constantly changing, but the foundational concepts will be here for good. Although year after year open rates and engagement are declining, I believe that email marketing is not going anywhere soon. There will always be some method of direct marketing with our followers. At most, email marketing will develop into a marginally different but similar enough mechanism that everything mentioned here will still apply.

For search engine optimization, algorithms change daily, but people will always need a way to find answers to their questions and discover new information. Although how that works could change dramatically (for example, voice search on smart devices is becoming increasingly common) getting our content in front of people organically with search engines isn't going away.

To better convey points, I've cited various third-party sources and will mention various statistics throughout the content. These numbers will fluctuate over time, and you should avoid interpreting them as perfectly current depending on when you're reading this. As much of a cop-out as it may sound, to find the most up-to-date data on anything mentioned here, simply perform a basic web search.

The first draft of this book didn't include any screenshots. I didn't want to have images of older interfaces that might in the future make the content seem like it was no longer relevant. However, I have added some because I feel many of the concepts are much easier to understand when I include screenshots of things such as Google search results and examples of proper web page design. So keep in mind, the underlying concepts of every image will remain evergreen, but the interfaces shown will inevitably change over time.

2. No Gimmicks, Exaggerations, or Over-Promising

I was at war with my editors as I finalized the cover and title for *Evergreen Affiliate Marketing*. Here's some of the feedback that I got on the title and cover.

"It needs more of a hook, it's a little dry . . ."

"You should tell people what they're going to get, like tips to earn $1,000/week passively."

"This looks like the type of book that I know I should read but it might be boring . . ."

These suggestions have merit. In terms of copywriting, they're absolutely correct. Adding more flare would absolutely help me sell more books more quickly. However, that's not my goal with *Evergreen Affiliate Marketing*. I've shared everything that I know is critical to affiliate marketing, and I want to "wow" you with the content so that the clickbait headlines won't be necessary to the long-term success of this book.

A quick stroll through Amazon will show you hundreds of books on affiliate marketing with catchy hooks and attractive promises. That isn't this book. This book promises one thing: to make you a better affiliate marketer. I won't make false guarantees like "earn $5,000/month passively from the beach" or "become a seven-figure marketer in thirty days." However, anyone who achieves these sorts of desirable outcomes absolutely leverages at least some tactics that you're going to learn in this book. You'll have the skills needed to do amazing things, but how you apply them and what the results are is entirely up to you.

3. This Book (Like All Affiliate Marketing Books) Is "Incomplete" and You Don't Need All of It Right Away (or Maybe Ever)

We're going to cover the heart of affiliate marketing, but it's not an "everything you need to succeed" type of guide. Because of the fluid nature of affiliate marketing, that sort of book isn't possible.

For example, at the time of this writing, Instagram stories with swipe up animations are working really well for my friends in the fitness industry. If you're reading this ten years after its original publication, Instagram may not even be around. The influencers who used that method will have pivoted to something else or left the industry entirely.

Most skills worth learning in the twenty-first century require ongoing learning. But don't worry, I cover how to ensure you stay up-to-date on the current state of affiliate marketing. I have an entire chapter titled " How to Learn What's Not in This Book," that is dedicated to ensuring you will be the most "in the know" affiliate marketer in every room you walk into.

As I mentioned already, part of what makes me uniquely qual- ified to write this book is the broad depth of experiences and extensive amount of different strategies I've used to reach my affil- iate marketing goals. I adopt an "omni-channel" and "omni-tac- tic" approach to making sales. While many affiliate marketers focus on one aspect, such as SEO or influencer type audience building, I have experimented and had success with most of the strategies out there.

Part of why I've done this is so I can document my experiences on my blog and YouTube channel. This has given me a unique advantage in discussing all the strategies at your disposal.

However, I don't recommend you follow in my footsteps in that regard. At least not right away. Some tactics, for example, will be more relevant to people who want to build big brands and followings. If this doesn't describe you, don't spend time on it. For this reason, you may find that reading this book a second or third time down the road is beneficial since your business will inevitably change and old content may become relevant.

4. You Won't Get a Sales Pitch

Last but not least, I promise that this isn't a cheap attempt at getting you into my sales funnel. A disturbing trend has started in recent years. As it became easier and more affordable to self-publish books, a lot of junk started popping up. No offense to self-publishers (this is a self-published book after all), but most of them would go into a shredder if the authors handed them to a major publisher.

Even worse, some of the most knowledgeable people in their fields attract readers off of their clout but then create books that hold back all of the useful substance. If an expert writes a book and withholds the best advice, they can't make a truly timeless and influential book. Instead, they turn their books into glorified sales letters that aim to sell you on an expensive upsell coaching program or course. This book is not that. I have no course on affiliate marketing, and I don't offer coaching. All I want to do is create the go-to resource for affiliate marketers and turn you into a lifelong follower of my free content on affiliate marketing and internet entrepreneurship.

You should be skeptical of every person in the "make money" online space (myself included). All I ask is that you read this book and decide for yourself if I'm just another marketer who makes money talking about marketing or if I'm the real deal and you can trust that I've given you the right strategies, tips, and tactics to make an impact in your life and business.

How to Read This Book

As I mentioned, this book is not a linear "A to Z" guide to affiliate marketing. I have, however, organized the chapters and ideas in a way that I believe is most logical and easy to follow. I've gone to great lengths to ensure that each chapter is as concise as possible without losing value. I've worked hard to make it easy to follow, even if you just picked up the book and flipped to a random page. The ideas in each chapter can stand by themselves, but you'll get the most value by reading the entire book.

The book is broken the book down into six sections.

1. Affiliate Marketing 101
2. Core Concepts and Mindset
3. Content Creation
4. Tactics and Strategy
5. Copywriting
6. Miscellaneous Thoughts and Considerations

In section 1 we go over the things that every new affiliate marketer needs to know. We will cover things such as how to find a great niche, how to choose which sort of traffic you will drive, and more.

I'm going to say this twice because it's important: **You can skip over this section if you're already an experienced affiliate mar-**

keter. I repeat, you can skip over this section if you're an experienced marketer.

The last thing that I want to do is bore you right out of the gate. Unfortunately, most people who purchase this book won't finish reading it. The completion rate for nonfiction books in 2021 is reportedly around 34%.[1] I'm going to make sure the content you do consume is meaningful, so please, don't spend time on this chapter if you don't need it.

In section 2 we go over the things that I feel you absolutely need to know. This is the only section that I highly recommend you read straight through. You're welcome and encouraged to read the rest of the book in any order that you like. Jump into the table of contents and start flipping to whatever concepts spark your interest, but I highly recommend that everyone reading this book reads the Core Concepts and Mindset section no matter what.

Don't worry, it's not a bunch of cheesy motivational fluff. It is full of the core concepts that I believe are the most important to your success as an affiliate marketer. If I removed everything else from this book except this chapter, it would give you a good framework to work with forever.

Section 3 covers content creation. All internet-based affiliate marketers create content. Even if you're the type of marketer who is only running anonymous paid ads to offers, you should know the evergreen content creation strategies. We cover content creation tactics and the general content creator mindsets that will make you a more confident creator.

Section 4 covers practical tactics and strategies. This will probably be your favorite section since it showcases many things that

---

1   Stephan Heyman, "Keeping Tabs on Best Seller Books and Reading Habits," *New York Times*, February 4, 2015, https://www.nytimes.com/2015/02/05/arts/international/keeping-tabs-on-best-seller-books-and-reading-habits.html.

you can implement immediately. While these aren't "secrets," I guarantee you will find at least a few new tactics that will make you want to drop the book and go implement them. Implementation of the tactics is far more important than reading about them, so if you're moved to take action, I want you to drop the book and do just that. The book will be here when you get back.

Section 5 covers copywriting. Copywriting is one of the most important skills an internet marketer can have. A 1,000-page book would barely scratch the service of everything there is to cover in the world of copywriting, so I cover just the things that I have found to be the most impactful concepts and tactics. This isn't a complete guide to copywriting, but it will give you the things I have seen to be most impactful.

Section 6 covers everything else that I wanted to share but didn't have a clear home in any of the first five sections. This section includes things I feel make the book "complete," and they read more like quick tips and advice rather than detailed chapters.

Last but not least, I've included a list of terms and definitions at the end of the book with key terms you should know. If you're relatively new to affiliate marketing, it may benefit you to read through those first so you can better follow along with the rest of the book. If you've been in the affiliate marketing space for a long time, you can skip this entirely. I put it at the end so as to not waste your time.

How to Learn What's Not in This Book

"Formal education will make you a living; self-education will make you a fortune."

—Jim Rohn

So by now we've established the fact that this book can't include all the methods that are working at the exact time that you're reading it. Fear not, though, I won't just leave you with no clue on how to fill the gaps and learn the specific trends and strategies that will come and go in your career.

Most of Affiliate Marketing is Constant

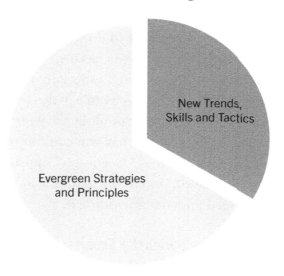

New Trends, Skills and Tactics

Evergreen Strategies and Principles

First, understand that the great affiliate marketers are lifelong learners. Even though I've written a book on affiliate marketing, if I stop learning, my businesses will slowly become less profitable. I'll lose out to the surrounding people who are keeping their thumb on the pulse of the industry—the people who are adapting to changes and constantly testing the old ways of doing things to make sure they still work.

Here are the core methods of learning affiliate marketing at the highest level.

Ongoing Learning Tactic #1: Google as You Go

In business school (something that is completely unnecessary to business success by the way) we learned about something called JIT inventory systems. Although one beauty of affiliate marketing is that you have zero inventory, we can learn from this inventory model.

JIT stands for "Just-In-Time" and it refers to an inventory management system in which companies increase efficiency and decrease waste by receiving goods only as they need them for the production process. In affiliate marketing, you'll regularly find yourself in situations where you need to learn how to do something.

As straightforward as this answer seems, Google is still the king for learning how to do anything, especially tech- or marketing-related tasks. Read tutorials or watch videos whenever you need to learn a new skill and you can fill in the gaps as you go.

Avoid over-learning new skills that you can't implement soon. Learning things with the "Google as you go" approach will give you exactly what you need, and you'll retain it at a higher level since you'll be engaged and actually doing it.

Ongoing Learning Tactic #2: Industry Experts

The commonsense place to learn about what's working in affiliate marketing is through the content of people like me who cover the affiliate marketing industry. This content is great, but it's so far from complete. It's not even a quarter of what you'll really need.

Ongoing Learning Tactic #3: General Mindfulness of the Marketing around You

While you should follow the influencers in the affiliate marketing space, limiting your learning to just that will leave you in the dark and in a race to the bottom. There's a saying in our industry, "Marketers ruin everything." If something is working, others will find out and they will beat it to the ground. Eventually, the methods become less effective or die out entirely. This leads to a massive race to the bottom where only the people willing to spend the most time and money on something will survive.

So the number one source of new information on what is working is to pay attention to the world around you. Notice the affiliate marketers who aren't gurus in the space. For example, I subscribe to very few YouTube channels and almost never "hit the bell." One creator shares stories about strange happenings and unsolved mysteries, and I hit the bell so I can follow everything he shares as soon as he shares it. He isn't an affiliate marketing guru, but he is a world-class affiliate marketer. Although I watch his channel for my entertainment, I've learned more about what's working in affiliate marketing right now from him than I have from almost anywhere else.

Ongoing Learning Tactic #4: Real-World Testing

"One learns from books and example only that certain things can be done. Actual learning requires that you do those things."
—Frank Herbert

You'll learn the most by simply trying new things consistently. Do more of what works and less of what doesn't. Allot a certain amount of time to "science" and try new things knowing that they likely will not pan out. Test out the latest social media platforms. A/B test every email subject line you send. Try different paid ad networks.

Let yourself give in a little to the "shiny object syndrome," and regularly test new methods. It's okay if it costs you some time and money—it's an investment in your own real-world education. It's always difficult for me to grasp how people will invest thousands on courses or coaching but become sticklers when they have to do something without guidance, like burning some money testing out paid ads before they're experts.

Get skin in the game early and often. You'll be shocked at how much more quickly you learn things when you have your own cash on the line. If you're in a raft and it's sinking, you'll come up with some creative ways to keep it afloat. The same is true for paid ads.

Now there's a fine line, of course, between doing research and letting yourself fall into distraction and unproductiveness. Don't let yourself fall into that, but never be afraid to allow yourself to test things.

Ongoing Learning Tactic #5: Tertiary Training (Platforms, Skills, and Tools)

Finally, a lot of what you'll need to learn won't relate directly to affiliate marketing. You won't always find all of this content in affiliate marketing blogs and forums. This includes things like taking a photo editing course, reading a book on the writing process, or watching a webinar about the latest Google algorithm updates.

Not everything worth learning will be labeled as clearly related to affiliate marketing. It's your job to fill in the gaps and develop and maintain the extra skills you need to succeed.

Ongoing Learning Tactic #6: Masterminds and Groups

Working for yourself doesn't mean you have to work by yourself. If for no other reason than to maintain your sanity, you should have a group of other affiliate marketers you connect with regularly. This can be in the form of a formal paid community or as informal as a group chat where you connect regularly with one another.

Don't be shy; you may be surprised at how friendly other people can be in the space. Great entrepreneurs know the power of networking and usually are more than open to connecting with other likeminded people.

Chapter Summary

- Successful affiliate marketing requires ongoing learning.
- We can find the best answers to questions for free online.
- Avoid over-learning if you can't apply skills soon. Instead, focus on just-in-time learning.
- Most of the experts in the affiliate marketing field give away their best information for free. Follow them.
- Be mindful of the marketing around you and emulate what is working.
- Test often and don't be afraid to fail. Learn from your mistakes.
- Not every valuable skill will relate directly to affiliate marketing. Learn the tertiary skills that make you more effective.
- Network with other affiliate marketers whether in a formal setting like a mastermind or an informal setting like a group chat.

Free Resources and Recommendations

I want to give you the best possible chance of succeeding with affiliate marketing. To help with this, I've created several free resources that will help you along your journey.

You can access these at any time at https://evergreenaffiliate-marketing.com/downloads. Current resources include the following:

- affiliate revenue planner
- bullet point worksheet
- topic research worksheet
- lead magnet checklist
- blog title worksheet
- blog post checklist
- blog update checklist

I update these regularly and if you remain on the email list, you'll receive an email when new resources are added.

Successful affiliate marketing leverages a lot of third-party software products and services. Because these change constantly, I can't mention many of them by name in this book. If you want to see what software products I'm currently using and recommending, visit https://evergreenaffiliatemarketing.com/tools.

AFFILIATE MARKETING 101

What Is Affiliate Marketing?

If you spent money on this book or took the risk involved to steal it (joking), it's likely that you have a basic understanding of what affiliate marketing is. To make sure that we leave no stone unturned, let's quickly go over what affiliate marketing actually is.

Affiliate marketing is a system of marketing in which third parties drive traffic and sales to the products of other companies in return for a commission. A commission is a percentage of sales or a flat rate that is paid after a successful sale and once any refund periods have expired.

Anything that can be sold can be sold via an affiliate program. Services, physical products, software, coaching, etc. If people buy it, there will be affiliate marketers who will promote it.

Affiliate marketing consists of three parties: the merchant, the advertiser, and the consumer.

The merchant is the owner of the product that the affiliate promotes. If an affiliate is promoting a company called Jim's Fishing Lures, Jim's Fishing Lures is the merchant. The merchant decide the terms of their affiliate program and which products they allow affiliates to promote. The advertiser is the affiliate marketer who sends traffic to Jim's Fishing Lures. Finally, you need a consumer to make everything work.

It's going to be extremely difficult for you to truly give affiliate marketing your all if you aren't proud of it. If you're embarrassed to be an affiliate marketer and feel the entire industry is rotten to the core, by all means, don't take part in it.

I mentioned already that the industry has far too many bad actors and people who care more about dollars than people. If you're afraid that you'll fall into that, return this book for a refund immediately and find a different career path. It's okay; it's not for everyone.

But before you give up, consider the following reasons why affiliate marketing is in fact a tremendous net positive for not only the marketers and product owners, but for the consumers as well.

1. Consumers Need Help Making Decisions

This may sound like I'm disrespecting the intelligence of the common person, but that isn't the case. I'm a consumer myself, and I rely on people I trust to give me good advice and direction.

We simply don't have enough time in the day to test and review every possible option for everything we buy and use. Sometimes we have to take a leap of faith and trust someone else's recommendation. This is why affiliate marketers are so great. They can help bring the best products to light and make the buying decision easier. This is assuming they are trustworthy (more on that in section 2 later), but consumers reward the most trustworthy marketers with repeat business.

Honest affiliates help confirm whether products are worth our time and money. The best affiliates develop trust, and consumers value having someone they trust to make buying decisions easier.

2. Consumers Get Tons of High-Quality Free Content

The internet would be a digital wasteland if it weren't for the incentive of money for creators. How many times have you searched Google or YouTube for something and had to pay for the answer? 99.99 percent of the time you didn't pay a cent.

But you may have unknowingly rewarded the creator by clicking on an ad or purchasing a product they recommend. If that didn't happen, we would all be paying for Google searches and information would come at a cost rather than be a luxury with an option to buy things that reward creators and cost us nothing extra.

3. Small Businesses Get to Leverage Risk-Free Advertising

Affiliate marketing is a catalyst for many small businesses. The product- or service-creators pay the marketer only after a sale or desired action has taken place. This means that small companies with limited budgets can grow tremendously fast even without much of their own marketing efforts or money for advertising.

If your affiliate marketing business is growing, you're helping other businesses grow as well. Unless the company has made a massive mistake on their affiliate structure, it is impossible for an affiliate to earn money without simultaneously earning money for the company they're endorsing.

4. Influencers (Affiliates) Get to Make Money Doing What They're Best at and NOT Spending Their Time Tied to a Single Business

Content creators can focus solely on their followers and the marketing of quality products. They can justify spending money on research and going the extra mile to create content that is of tremendous value.

Affiliate marketers can focus on creating free content around passion topics and still monetize without asking their followers for a dime with relevant and valuable products.

You should be proud to be a cog in the machine of affiliate marketing. When done correctly, it is a huge net positive for companies, consumers, and promoters. You don't have to "sell out" to make sales, and you can sleep well at night knowing that you aren't just making money but you're making a positive difference in the lives of the people fortunate enough to run across your content.

Chapter Summary

- Affiliate marketing is a form of marketing that involves a merchant (the product owner), an advertiser (the affiliate promoting the product), and a consumer to purchase from them.
- Affiliate marketing is a tremendous value to small business owners because they get to leverage risk-free marketing since they only pay when a sale is made.

- Consumers benefit from affiliate marketing because marketers are encouraged to create highly valuable, free content.

The Four Affiliate Approaches

There is no cookie-cutter affiliate marketer. If something makes affiliate commissions, it's affiliate marketing and the person getting paid is an affiliate marketer. There are, however, several broad buckets that most affiliate marketers fall into.

Just as with choosing the medium you use for exposure, choosing your approach is a Yin/Yang decision. Choosing just one can limit your results, and choosing all of them out of the gate can spread your efforts too thin to see results.

The ideal approach is to choose one style first and let it play out. Once you've seen results, you can consider adding new styles.

Style #1. Paid Traffic

A Catch-22 method, this is the easiest way to get started making money with affiliate marketing, but it also requires that you have some money to spend. The ability to buy attention has changed the way we do business in the twenty-first century, and media buying is here to stay.

This method is not for the faint of heart. It requires patience and a learner's mindset. To find lasting success with paid traffic, you need to adopt a mentality of lifelong learning. If you master a certain network, it will change. Those who don't adapt quickly lose their profitability.

Style #2. SEO

The idea of "free traffic," makes SEO (search engine optimization) an extremely attractive method. However, the method is far from free. Although you won't be spending much in terms of dollars, the time and effort required to truly drive organic traffic can be tremendous.

Also, having money to spend is still a tremendous advantage since you can hire experts to build links, write content, and improve SEO. Just like paid traffic, SEO requires a commitment to continual learning. Search engines are continually updating their algorithms to prevent marketers from gaming the system. Since traffic is money, marketers will always find and exploit every loophole available and search engines will always plug the holes with updates.

Style #3. Influencer

If you're a people person, the influencer approach can be a tremendous option. The biggest benefit is that you'll create trust with your followers. People buy from people they know, like, and trust, so the conversion rates influencers will experience is typically much higher than any other method.

This approach can be mentally draining and isn't for anyone who worries about dealing with negative comments online. If you sell things, someone will have issues with it. If you're able to ignore that, this approach is golden.

With few exceptions, it can take quite some time to build a following. If you're ready to make that commitment, this method might be for you.

Style #4. Passive Referrer

One method that most people completely overlook, this strategy involves recommending relevant products to customers of a traditional business or service. One of the most successful affiliate marketers I've ever met uses this approach to sell recurring software to clients of his gym set-up service.

I've implemented all four of these styles now into my business, but I started with organic traffic/SEO.

Chapter Summary

- There are four types of affiliate marketers, but you can be more than one type at a time.
- Sales can be made by attracting organic visitors, running paid traffic, growing a large following on social media, or passively referring products that are relevant to your other businesses.

Finding Your Niche

There are several "boxes" that need to be checked when validating a niche to pursue. I highly recommend that you make sure that your niche checks all of them before you invest the time, energy, and money into pursuing it further.

Remember, you will invest a lot of time and energy into this process, so you want to get this part right! Here are the factors that make a niche worth pursuing as an affiliate.

Niche Requirement #1. An Audience That Is Willing and Able to Spend Money

It doesn't matter how much content or value you create if the audience you serve can't eventually buy something. You are investing time, energy, and money into this, so it's necessary that you get something in return. If you want to create what I call a "digital diary" and never make a penny, good for you. This book applies to people who are looking at content creation as a source of revenue. It can and should also provide personal satisfaction and fulfillment, but *revenue is key*.

Niche Requirement #2. An Audience That Is Large Enough to Fulfill Your Goals

Just because there is a niche that is able and willing to buy from you doesn't mean that it is big enough to merit your time. Set big goals and make sure you don't jump into a niche that has a low ceiling for opportunity.

Niche Requirement #3. A Market That Is Well Defined and Not Saturated

You've most likely heard the saying, "There are riches in the niches." As the internet expands, niches that once performed become flooded with competition. What was once a profitable niche for the early adopters can become diluted by competitors, and profits decrease exponentially.

So what makes something "saturated"? This depends, but the best way to find which markets are saturated and should be avoided is with third-party tools. Some are free and some will cost money. I will get into this process shortly. Just keep in mind as you go through the process that a niche needs to have people who will buy and is defined enough that you can actually get a piece of the market without investing years into creating content.

Niche Requirement #4. Covers a Topic That You Are Passionate about and Interested In

Some articles write this factor as "optional," but for me, it is mandatory. Everyone has something they are passionate about. There IS profit in your passions somewhere if you look hard enough, I promise. It's not always easy, but you will be thrilled that you took the time and energy here on the front end. Again, it takes passion to create commitment, and it takes commitment to create great content, and it takes great content to create affiliate income.

Some of you can get by on your rock solid passion of the process. (I admit, I can write about almost anything and still stay excited because the process of internet marketing excites me on its own.) But 99% of people need to be passionate about their topic in order to stick with it. You will also find that content just pours out of you when you're interested in it. Your readers will know if you're passionate or not, and passion sells!

Here are three steps for researching whether or not an affiliate niche is worth pursing.

Research Strategy #1. Review Top Websites

At the time of this writing, I use a tool called Quantcast to show me the most popular sites online. This is a great place to start if you're in the brainstorming phase. Don't worry about the big pages on the top 100. We can't realistically emulate those. More power to you if you want to try, but that isn't in the spirit of what I teach.

You're going to look at the sites further down. I recommend starting at around 10,000 rank. Pay attention to the niches that appear. Sites ranked this high are generating revenue. If they aren't, the owners are doing something wrong or are organizations that are looking to build awareness rather than make money, such as social justice movements.

Research Strategy #2. Review Affiliate Products from Major Affiliate Networks

There will always be large affiliate networks that connect products with promoters. These networks can be a great place to find inspiration not just on what to promote, but what niches to pursue.

I have discovered a lot of niche site ideas simply from the affiliate products I saw listed on a large network around at the time of this writing called ClickBank. One example is an affiliate program for an info product that includes hundreds of blueprints for woodworking projects.

Example Affiliate Research

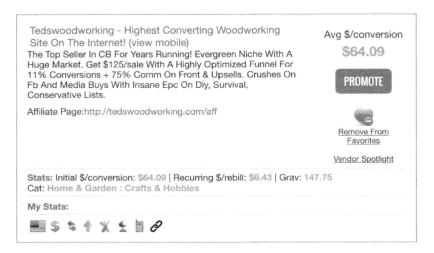

Seeing this may inspire you to create content related to this niche. Again, this exercise isn't about finding a product to promote just yet, but if you find something that you think could be your core product and you could create content for it, by all means, pursue it!

Research Strategy #3. Look at Cost-Per-Click Data in Major Search Engines

People don't spend money on keywords that don't make money. At least not for very long. At the time of this writing, I'm using the basic keyword planner tool provided by Google. This shows estimated costs to run ads to various search terms.

Most pay-per-click programs have a massive amount of features, filters, and functions. There are people who dedicate their lives to mastering them. Don't become overwhelmed by the array of options. For this exercise, you only need to concern yourself with the keyword planner. The higher the cost per click, the more affiliate offers and affiliate options you will have.

This process is simple, but it takes a lot of work. Don't rush niche selection! Choose a topic that you can see yourself creating content in for some time to come. Finding that nice overlap of passion and financial incentive is what this process is all about.

Chapter Summary

- Choosing the wrong niche will destroy your chances of success, even with excellent execution and hard work.
- A great niche should have an audience that is willing and able to spend money, have an audience that is large enough to scale, be in a market that isn't saturated, and be a topic of extreme interest to you.
- Finding a niche that you're passionate about isn't mandatory, but it makes it much easier to stick with the process and create great content.
- You can analyze the profitability of a niche by seeing what advertisers are paying for clicks in search engines.

Audio vs. Video vs. Writing

Choosing how you'll get your message out to the world (and eventually get paid for it) is a big decision. This chapter will help you decide which content medium is best for you. I'm going to argue the case for each of the main three content mediums: the written word (blogs), audio (podcasts), and video (YouTube). If you've already chosen a medium and have established yourself on it, you're welcome to skip this chapter.

One thing to keep in mind while reading this chapter is that social media platforms can fall into or in between any of these mediums. For instance, platforms like Twitter lean more toward writing first but also include video or audio content.

This chapter doesn't involve these platforms. It is perfectly normal and recommended to create and maintain the basic social media channels relevant to your industry. You can choose to focus on writing as your core medium and build your blog while also occasionally tweeting and maintaining your blog's fan page on Facebook. Likewise, you can focus on YouTube and maintain a casual presence on whatever other big social media platform is common. You should build your social media platforms from day one, regardless of whether you choose audio, video, or writing as your core medium.

Although there are pros and cons for each, I highly recommend that you start with only one of these mediums. In a perfect world, we'd have a large, active presence across all three mediums right out of the gate. No matter what your message is, there are people who would prefer to consume it by listening, reading, or viewing. So being on more platforms allows you to reach and help more people. You can do that in time, but it's optimal to start with a linear focus.

The Catch-22 of specialization is that putting all of our eggs in one basket can lead to the total collapse of our businesses when things change (which they inevitably will). Going too broad is just as bad, though, so we need to find a solution in the middle.

Successful, career-minded affiliate marketers balance the need to separate themselves from the herd through specialization without setting themselves up for total destruction when platforms disappear or strategies stop working. Perry Marshall calls this the "YinYang" of Media Expertise in his classic book *80/20 Sales and Marketing*.[2] The Yin being our need to focus and the Yang being our need to ensure our entire business is not dependent on one source of traffic or one advertising medium.

Putting all of the eggs in one basket isn't any better than spreading yourself too thin. Specialize first and then create balance for support.

Each medium has its own unique set of skills you need to develop. There will be a slow growth phase as you start followed by an exponential spike in growth once you reach a critical amount of traction. James Clear, author of New York Time's best seller Atomic Habits describes this best with his concept of "the plateau of latent potential."[3]

---

2 Perry Marshall, *80/20 Sales and Marketing: The Definitive Guide to Working Less and Making More* (Irvine, CA: Entrepreneur Press, 2013).
3 James Clear, *Atomic Habits* (New York: Penguin Random House, 2018), 21–23.

The Plateau of Latent Potential

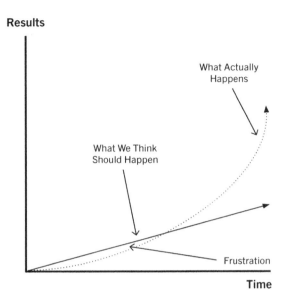

All things being equal, if we divide our time equally between all three mediums, it will take much longer to grow any one platform. One year spent focusing linearly on one medium will almost always produce greater results than if you were to divide the time among each medium. We should focus on one medium first and then use that audience to help expedite the growth of the others (if you choose to expand to others). Focus here is a growth hack while diversifying too soon is only going to slow you down.

This decision is hard because all the big names in every space seem to use all three mediums at once. However, most of them started with just one and then used that audience to increase the speed of growth for their other platforms. By definition, fewer people will ever notice the early stages of an influencer's career, so it's hard to appreciate that they likely started slowly.

"One Feeds Many" Platform Model

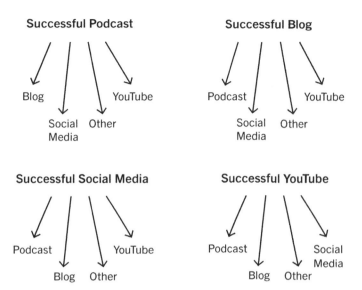

Pat Flynn, one of the first influencers in the affiliate marketing space, used his podcast to grow his website and email list. He then used that to grow his large YouTube channel at a breakneck speed. You can find countless examples of influencers who started on one medium and then leveraged their audience to quickly grow in others.

This chapter could be extremely short if there was a one-size-fits-all answer to "which medium is best for affiliate marketing?" There isn't. You can find wildly successful people in any of the three mediums. The question you should ask instead is, "Which platform is best for me right now?"

Let's start by comparing each medium in key areas: conversions, engagement, ease of creation, and ease of growth. These are generalizations and results can vary. There are extreme outliers, but these are the things I've seen to be true in my decade of affiliate marketing.

Writing Is the Best Medium for Conversions

Blogs are best for conversions because they have limitless potential for adding calls to action. You can sell products, collect emails, and drive any sort of desired action at the same time on the same page. Blogging is also the only medium where the tool of taking action (the mouse or touch screen) is actively being used. For audio and video platforms, you need to compel your viewer or listener to take an action. This means they have to do extra work. However, conversion rates will typically be much higher from traffic sent via podcasts and video since the visitor has shown they are serious enough to go out of their way to visit the product you recommended. Podcast listeners will most likely have to literally type the URL into their browser bar, and video viewers also have to do extra work to find the calls to action in descriptions or call-outs. The volume of clicks you get from blogs, however, will generally offset the lower conversion rates.

I've purchased many products from podcasts, and I totally expect an ad or two during a show. Smart podcasters know to get some sort of branded and easy-to-remember offer code that will attribute sales to them since they will miss out on the cookie attribution from direct clicks. Again, conversion rates will be through the roof when people do put in the work to convert, but the total number of impressions will be the lowest of the three mediums.

For video, my experience has been that people don't appreciate being sold things on YouTube as much as they do on other mediums. You can link to products in cards (if they're on your owned and approved website) or in the description, but it is not nearly as easy to get traffic off the platform and to your desired pages.

Video Is the Best Medium for Engagement

Video gets by far the most engagement of the three mediums. Viewers can leave comments and expect replies to them quickly.

Real discussions happen in the YouTube comment section, and viewers are used to that so they comment even more. The downside to this is filtering out spam comments, but the reward is typically well worth the price.

Popular blogs can receive a good amount of comments, but there is a mild barrier to entry and a longer delay between comments and comment interaction. Most blogs require verification and a user account to leave a comment. This added step causes many would-be commenters to not bother.

Besides reviews, podcasts don't have a good way for the viewer to engage with episodes. To truly drive engagement, podcasters need to send their listeners to their other social media platforms. This is extra work but is well worth the effort.

Audio Is the Easiest Medium to Quickly Create Content

Although some expert podcasters will argue this, I believe podcasting is the easiest sort of content to produce. You can create high-quality podcasts on a tiny budget. If you're like me, you'll tolerate lower quality audio if the substance is great. As you scale, you can upgrade your gear, hire editors, and improve production quality, but the barrier to entry is very low. You can crank out dozens of podcasts in a very short amount of time.

Creating blog content isn't incredibly difficult. Yes, my opinion means less since I've written hundreds of posts in my life, but it's really not as hard as many people make it out to be. The learning curve isn't incredibly steep, and once a repeatable process is created, you can produce a great deal of content in a short amount of time.

With video content, unless you have experience with editing or have a rough, minimalistic style that requires little to no editing, video content can be a huge time suck. As you scale, you can optimize and outsource this process, but it is still laborious. I've found that I take about two to three times as long to film and edit a video than I take to write a 1,500+ word blog post.

Video Is the Easiest Medium to Grow an Audience

YouTube is by far the fastest medium to get views, and every video-based social media platform that has launched in the past decade has seen quick growth. Video-based platforms don't seem to play favorites quite like search engines do either. They'll gladly send huge amounts of traffic to new channels if they create great content and follow some basic best practices. Authority and longevity are less of a factor most of the time. If you have a video that is getting a high average watch time and good engagement, you can quickly appear atop search results for very competitive search terms.

Although it can take a while to grow domain authority and rank in search engines for competitive terms, bloggers who understand how to perform proper keyword research can start getting visitors much more quickly than people may think. This takes practice, though, and most bloggers don't figure out how to properly drive traffic with low competition topics until they've written a lot of posts that didn't get traction.

With podcasts, unless you hit the "New and Noteworthy," or "What's Hot" sections or have an existing following, growing your podcast audience is a slow march. Episodes can be created quickly, but getting people to listen to them is a different struggle. One of the big benefits, though, is that once you hook someone on your podcast, they are likely to binge your earlier episodes. This means that one fan can end up consuming way more content than they typically would on YouTube or a blog. This lets you build a relationship with them quickly and allows you to expose them to your cornerstone affiliate product quickly and often.

Pros and Cons of Blogging

Pros:

✔ 100% ownership and no one can take it from you or ban you from it.

✔ Leverage the power of Google and other search engines for free organic traffic.

✔ Increase the visibility of calls to action and list building assets.

✔ Pixel and retarget traffic for increased conversions.

✔ Content creation is relatively fast (most bloggers report spending less than 3.5 hours to publish a single post).

✔ Avoid the need to show your face or share your voice.

✔ Turning off commenting doesn't dramatically harm your traffic.

✔ Limitless content updating keeps things current and fresh.

Cons:

✖ Need to learn to play the SEO game in order to rank content in a timely fashion.

✖ Can take a long time to build up domain authority and compete in search engines.

✖ The written word is not trending upward in consumer preferences for content consumption.

✖ Less engagement (on average) than video but more than podcasts.

Pros and Cons of Video

Pros:

✔ The most popular form of content consumption.

✔ Monetize via display ads in addition to any other desired methods.

✔ Pixel and retarget traffic for increased conversions.

✔ Huge viewer engagement in the comments section.

✔ Video content is shared most frequently.

Cons:

✘ YouTube isn't as natural a sales channel (people don't love to be sold on YouTube).

✘ Creating videos typically takes much longer and requires editing skills that don't come naturally to many people.

✘ YouTube can ban your channel overnight (you don't own it).

✘ Limitations in updating old videos with new information.

Pros and Cons of Audio

Pros:

✔ Encourage listeners to "binge" your content.

✔ Subtle ads can have massive conversion rates.

✔ Pixel and retarget traffic for increased conversions.

✔ Content creation is relatively fast.

✔ Become a highly sought-after commodity as people want to be guests on your show.

✔ The number of podcast listeners is growing, from 18% of the US population in 2008 to 44% in 2018.

Cons:

✘ Conversions require more work from the listener (navigating to a website and entering promo code).

✘ Massive amounts of competition.

✘ Little to no organic search traffic.

✘ Reviews can dramatically increase or decrease number of listeners.

✘ Far less engagement (typically requires third-party social media to really engage with followers).

✘ Difficult to update older uploads.

There are pros and cons to each medium. The one you choose should be based on your unique personality and which medium will allow you to reach the most people as quickly as possible. Choose the medium that you like best and remember that you can (and should) expand to other platforms later.

Chapter Summary

- There is no single "best" medium.
- It is optimal to expand into all three mediums over time, but you should always start with only one.
- If you grow a large following on one medium, it becomes much easier to grow on other platforms by cross promoting to your existing audience.

Four Traffic Types

There are four types of traffic, but none of them are free. Anyone who says they're getting "free traffic" is forgetting to mention the work they put in to get it. Sure, some traffic is far less expensive or requires much less work, but there is always some form of time commitment. Think of any example of traffic you like and we can always tie it back to time or money. Here are some examples.

4 Types of Traffic

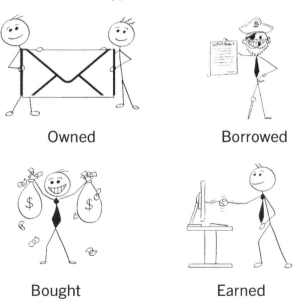

Owned

Borrowed

Bought

Earned

Traffic Source: An influencer shared your blog post and sends 10,000 clicks.

Cost: You made content worth sharing. You built a reputation that made you someone they were happy to be associated with. Traffic Source: A search engine shows your article for 800 keyword searches and you get 2,000 clicks a month to that article.

Cost: Time creating content. Time optimizing content. Basic web costs. Educational costs or time spent learning how to get blog posts written and ranked.

Traffic Source: A video you shared goes viral and drives traffic to your homepage where people want to learn more about you.

Cost: Time creating video. Time spent creating all other videos that didn't drive traffic.

You see what I'm getting at here? Time is more important than money. Why is it, then, that so many people will call something "free" when it takes a lot of time and effort to achieve? Whether you have a good idea of how much your time is worth or not, you'll be passing up on a lot of earning potential if you decide to focus your time on building organic traffic. It's also probably going to take much longer than you expect to get real organic traffic.

> **Hofstadter's Law:** "It always takes longer than you expect, even when you take into account Hofstadter's Law."

Hofstadter's Law is very true in growing organic traffic. It is not free. You earn it and buy it with time and effort. Unfortunately, organic traffic isn't a "set it and forget it" arrangement. If you have a blog post that is driving 1,000 organic visits per month, you'll have competitors aiming to take your spot. Search traffic is usually a worthwhile investment, but it is far from free and it isn't easy.

Not all traffic is created equal, and there are an endless number of ways to get it. No matter what, the number one goal is almost always to grow your owned traffic. This is a never-ending process, and that is extremely exciting. All things being equal, the more traffic you drive, the more money you can earn. Obviously, there are other factors involved such as the quality and relevance of the traffic, but the concept remains the same. Drive more of the same quality traffic and you'll earn as much money as you want. There is no cap on this, and that keeps the most successful affiliate marketers engaged and motivated long after they've earned a great deal of money.

At the time of this writing, email is still the number one source of owned traffic. Although the days of 70% open rates and 20% CTRs (click through rates) are no longer the norm, email marketing is still highly effective and will remain that way for the foreseeable future. Eventually, it may be overtaken by something slightly different, but there will always be some source of "owned" traffic. You'll know it when and if it changes from email, but whatever it is, amass as much of it as possible. But what is "owned traffic?"

Owned Traffic: An audience you can reach at any time through properties you have complete control over. This includes email, snail mail, SMS, and any other customer contact information that you have the legal right to contact. This audience can come and go as they please (they will), but except for some serious future legal intervention and government policy changes, no one can take this from you.

Owned traffic, however, requires us to dip our toes into the other types of traffic first. There are three major types of traffic we don't own but use. We will discuss owned traffic further in the next two chapters.

Borrowed Traffic: Any traffic we receive by being a part of a medium that we don't control. If you can be banned from it, it's borrowed traffic. Social media platforms and public forums are borrowed traffic since someone can take away or throttle your reach at any time and for any reason. Although the traffic and exposure is just as valuable when you get it, it's not as reliable and we shouldn't rely on them completely. We need to balance borrowed traffic with traffic that we have more control over or we risk losing our income streams overnight.

Bought Traffic: Any traffic we purchase through third parties. This can include paid promotions from influencers, search engine ads, display ads, and social media ads. We can purchase as much of this traffic as we like. We can pay for impressions, views, clicks, or engagement. Tracking our paid ad conversions with affiliate marketing isn't always possible because many vendors do not allow their affiliates to install tracking software on their landing pages. Some platforms, however, make this possible, and we should always track conversions if we can.

Earned Traffic: This is traffic that you get by "working your way in." Examples include things like going on podcasts where the host has you tell their listeners how they can learn more about you and you send them to your website. This can also take the form of any "guerrilla marketing" you use such as hosting in-person events and passing out business cards with your information.

Chapter Summary

- There are four types of traffic: owned, borrowed, bought, and earned.
- Owned traffic is by far the most valuable, but it requires the other forms of traffic first to build.

The Expert's Dilemma and the Dunning Kruger Effect

"Ignorance more frequently begets confidence than does knowledge."

—Charles Darwin

I was twenty-two when I wrote my first real blog post. I cringe thinking about the overt, unmerited confidence I wrote with. You'd have thought I was a savvy millionaire who had seen and done it all. In reality, I was a cocky kid who had made a few thousand dollars doing one thing and thought I was the next Elon Musk. These weren't opinion pieces, these were "this is how it is" types of posts.

Little did I know how little I knew. I still had countless numbers of massive mistakes to make—things that would mold me into something much closer to an expert and open my eyes to how naive I really was.

As I started to realize how little I knew, I found myself sharing less and less. I started to read and listen more and write more about my personal experiences than what I believed were absolute truths. Now I feel confident I have a strong but imperfect understanding of the internet business arena. Shockingly, I still am not as confident as I was back in year number one.

This is the Dunning-Kruger effect, and it's not uncommon, especially among content creators. In the field of psychology, the

Dunning-Kruger effect is a cognitive bias that people with a low competence in a task frequently overestimate their ability while people with higher competence frequently underestimate their ability.

The Dunning Kruger Effect

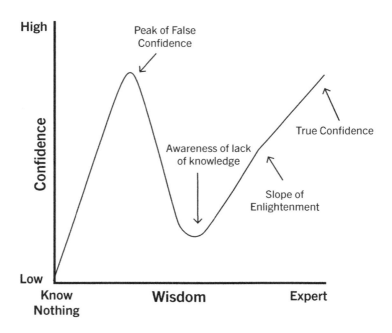

One of the great misconceptions among content creators is that we assume people will only listen to us if we have all the answers. In reality, that's simply not the case. Misguided creators do things that don't benefit their followers and damage their trust with them.

- They create courses on topics they've had only minimal success with themselves.
- They write blog posts exposing "truths" that they'll change their opinions on in the near future.

- They speak in absolutes before they've really tried alternatives.

We don't need to do this. Here's how to fight the Dunning Kruger effect.

First, besides the cringe factor later on, I see no real harm in falling victim to the Dunning-Kruger effect early on in your career. It's perfectly normal and, luckily, you won't have a huge audience right out of the gate to see this early cringe content. I'd argue that falling victim to the Dunning-Kruger effect and exuding overconfidence is better than falling victim to imposter syndrome and never sharing anything at all.

However, if you're new and want to avoid it, here's how. It's about being selective with what we discuss and how we discuss it. For example, I could start a blog about gardening, even though I'm not a gardener. I could also do this without "faking it until I make it." How? By sharing my story and experiences.

- "Inside My First Attempt at Growing Beets"
- "Here's How I Just Killed My Tomatoes"
- "The Five Plants I'm Most Excited to Try to Grow"

You see? Those are all very interesting topics BUT they don't feign expertise. They don't have to. So instead of assuming you have to adopt the persona of the "expert" or "guru," consider adopting the persona of the tester or documentarian.

Being an expert in your field should be your ultimate goal. Becoming an expert is a byproduct of years of dedication, commitment, application, and mistakes.

What defines an expert is up for interpretation. We live in the age of information, so being a true expert requires ongoing learning and is a continual process rather than a state of being.

Now you may be thinking to yourself, "Okay . . . becoming an expert is the goal, that's not worth a blog post, Nate." But wait, there is much, much more to this. This chapter has a very important message for anyone who serves a demographic or niche (software developers, content creators, etc.). This message is so important, in fact, that it could quite literally change your business forever.

If I hadn't followed the advice I am about to give to you, I wouldn't have accomplished anything yet. I wouldn't have provided the content, products, and services that have helped thousands of people in my market and made me a good living as a result.

While becoming an "expert" in your field should be your ultimate goal, what you do with the time leading up to this level of experience is critically important. How you handle yourself before you are well-known as a leading expert will have a huge impact on your business success and credibility throughout your career.

Please take the next line very seriously and trust me (it is the core of my business model and I promise you, it is true): You don't need to be an expert in your field to serve your target market immediately, and you do need to be an expert at something, but that doesn't mean you need to know everything in your field.

Okay, here is what you need to understand: You need to become an expert on the problems and needs of your audience. You can't help others without knowing what their problems are. I'm not referring to just the obvious ones (although low-hanging opportunities are frequently overlooked by competitors and there may be opportunity here). I am referring to acquiring a deep understanding of the following:

- What wastes your target customer's time?
- What causes your target customer to lose money?
- What causes your target customer to become frustrated?

- What is your target customer's biggest fear?
- What does your target customer value?
- What opportunities are your target customers overlooking?
- What does the future look like for your target customer?

You should also know the answers to some of the questions about:

- What solutions already exist?
- What do they do well?
- What are they lacking?
- Why do people use them over other options?
- What do your target customers love about the existing solutions?
- What do your target customers hate about the existing solutions?
- Are the prices on these other solutions too high or too low?

Asking and answering the questions above requires both empathy and creativity (two of the traits I respect most in people). Test the current solutions for yourself. Literally buy them, try them, read them, whatever you need to do. I buy and try a lot of things in my process of identifying needs for my target customers. I often learn a lot in the process from my potential competitors. Oh, and don't be a jerk; if you buy something from a competitor just to check it out, don't return it. That is tacky and ethical affiliate marketers are above that.

When you are an expert in your field, you may no longer suffer as many potential problems as a novice or even the majority of others in your field. You begin to focus on higher-level problems (ones that many in your field don't even know about yet). This can become limiting if your goal is to service that market and see things holistically.

An expert can begin to lose empathy with the typical member of their market. They no longer share as many of the same problems as someone with less experience. The truth is, these are frequently the people who need to be served the most. Regardless of the niche, there are more people who aren't experts. If you cater only to people on your level of expertise, you can limit your potential to truly help a great number of people at the highest level.

When you are an expert, you have an opportunity to help your market on a larger scale, but you will be limited greatly if you lose empathy for others facing different experiences. Quite often this is the case, which is why this chapter needed to be included in this book.

There is quite often a disconnect between having a lot of experience in a field and the ability to create products that serve it. Many great products (services, software, etc.) are created by a member of a market who identified a problem, corrected it, and had the audacity to share it in spite of lacking massive credibility. There is no better way to boost your credibility than by creating something that serves the community well.

I have eight brothers and sisters. Aside from DNA, most of us McCallisters share a common personality trait: sarcasm. It isn't exactly a beautiful character trait, but sarcasm can be a hilarious way to make a point.

My sister Anna is arguably the best at expressing sarcasm, flinging subtle sarcastic darts that cut your ego straight to the core. Although I am typically a very confident person, I admit that I give my words an extra second or two of thought before I say them around her. This must be a conditioned response from past sarcastic burns that were the emotional equivalent of being karate chopped in the throat.

Sarcastic people fight the urge to view the world with a "what is wrong here" approach. When channeled correctly, this is perfectly conducive to identifying problems. In business, the word "problem" is synonymous with "opportunity." You have an advantage over others if you decide to approach things by asking yourself, "What is missing here?" Or, "How is this not perfect?"

Now, being negative and not leveraging it for improvements and change but merely as a reason to complain makes you, well, a bit of a douchebag. Self-help books typically suggest we change the way we see things—that we train our minds to see things in a positive light. I'm not sure if this really works or not (to me, how you see things is more about brain chemistry than some adjustable mentality, but I am no neuroscientist. Either way, whether we can change how we see things or not, we can change the way we respond to them quite easily. Do this!

I will be the first to admit that I don't consider myself an expert in everything related to internet entrepreneurship. I am not an expert at copywriting, e-commerce, outsourcing, or anything that I teach at EntreResource. There is simply too much that I know I don't know yet.

"Then why the hell are you writing so much!?" you may be wondering.

Although I don't know everything, everything that I say, I believe to be true. I feel this way because I have experienced it, researched it, and considered all other options known to me. The points I make are based on facts, experiences, and testing.

Even if I did know everything, there isn't enough time to cover it all. I have plenty of valuable information to share as it is. You do too. Just make this promise to yourself: If you don't know something, accept that you just don't know. Never let your desire to be seen as an expert cause you to give advice that you aren't sure is sound. This is how you lose credibility, not by not having all the answers but by proving you are too dumb (usually just too proud) to know (or admit) that you don't know.

Chapter Summary

- The Dunning Kruger effect is a cognitive bias that people with a low competence in a task frequently overestimate their ability while people with higher competence frequently underestimate their ability.
- The Dunning Kruger effect is very typical in the world of content creation. Embrace the fact that you will likely cringe when you look back at your early content. This is far better than imposter syndrome.
- You don't need to be an expert to share amazing content. There are many different approaches to content creation that don't require being the all-knowing guru in your space.

Grow Your Owned Traffic

I've worked very hard to maintain the "evergreen" nature of everything I've written in this book, but I'm going to take a leap of faith here. I'm going to assume that email isn't going away in my lifetime and that growing your email list will continue to be paramount to affiliate marketing success.

The rate of effectiveness changes over time, so I won't throw out numbers here about open rates, conversion rates, etc. Just know, it will always work. Yes, it's not the year 2000 when people hadn't yet learned about spam and were still naïve enough to think they really won a free cruise if they got an email saying they did. We aren't getting 70% open rates, but that's perfectly fine. Consumers expect to be sold things in emails, and that will not change any time in our lifetime.

In the most extreme scenario, email will get a facelift and become something slightly different. Regardless, there will always be some means of collecting your potential buyer's information and having permission to contact and solicit to them.

The saying that "the money is in the list," is true at the time of this writing and will be true whenever you're reading it. What that list is called might change, but the concept will remain.

An engaged, targeted email list is the ultimate affiliate marketing asset. It is something that you own that can't be taken away from you. It lets you reach potential customers with no additional costs (beyond the subscription to the software that allows you to send mass messages).

List building is a beautiful thing because you can get extremely creative with it. There are hundreds of effective and legal strategies to grow your list. I will not spend time in this book going through all the different strategies. Instead, I'll explain the process as succinctly as possible.

Every strategy comes back to some exchange of value. Emails are not "free," and you can't expect people to hand them over to you. Just like you wouldn't expect someone to give you a $5 bill because you stick your hand out, you shouldn't expect emails for nothing in return. Here are some tips that will help you get more high-quality leads.

A quick nIte, the tiIs I'm about to share apply mostly to your own website. I highly recommend that all affiliate marketers have their own website, even if they aren't using SEO as a source of traffic. If you're an influencer on social media, you should have a website to send your visitors to so they can become email subscribers. At the very least, you need to have your own landing pages created that turn other forms of traffic into owned traffic.

Lead Generation Tip #1. Always Be Testing

"Never stop testing, and your advertising will never stop improving."

—David Ogilvy

The first attempt at anything will never be the most optimized. Everything you create can be made better and we do that by regularly testing and experimenting with new approaches. We will cover this in much greater detail in the chapter "Testing the Right Way."

Be sure to test one element at a time so you understand what is causing changes in conversions. You do this by using A/B testing, which is discussed in the chapter "Testing the Right Way."

With lead magnets, the more the merrier. I try to create lead magnets that cover every sub-niche that my blog attracts, and I try to create different media types to resonate with the most readers possible. I don't care if a subscriber prefers PDFs, audio files, or workbooks just as long as they are interested in the things I share and could be a valuable member of my email list.

More lead magnets also means better segmentation and targeting later. I can create segments and tags that make sure I don't send emails to people who wouldn't care about them. (See the chapter "The Email Tags You Should Use.") The more emails I send that aren't relevant to the recipient, the more unsubscribes I get and the less money I make in the long run.

Lead Generation Tip #2. Aggressively Segment

We want to ensure that we optimize our display rules. This means showing the right lead magnets to the right readers at the right time. The mechanics of how this works varies, but any lead generation software worth using will offer this sort of functionality. For example, if your website covers two sub-topics, you'd want to show a different lead magnet for each of them. Increase the relevance of the lead magnet based on the segmentation and you'll increase conversions.

Lead Generation Tip #3. Be Aggressive

According to Embertribe.com, almost 95% of people who visit

your site will never return. Let that sink in. When you realize how slim your chances are of turning traffic into long-term followers, you'll spend much more time and energy on your lead magnets and optimization.

If you're afraid of pop-ups annoying your readers, don't be. You may think to yourself, "But Nate, I hate pop-ups. Why would I use them on my site if they annoy me so much?" I struggled with this at first too. Remember this: You aren't your readers. What annoys you may not annoy them.

Many people love pop-ups if it sends them to something that helps them. Want your pop-ups to be less annoying? Create better lead magnets! People forget all about intrusive pop-ups if they end with them receiving something outstanding.

I use this analogy when explaining the art of giving in marketing and why it is the only way to actually find lasting success in the business. Pretend you're walking down the street and a homeless man pops out of nowhere and says, "Hey! Can I have some money!?!?" That would be super annoying, right? The odds of you giving him money are next to zero. If you give him money, it's likely because you're afraid of him and you're going to avoid walking down that street in the future.

Now pretend that the same homeless man pops out when you're walking down the street and says, "Hey! You don't want to keep walking this direction, there's a pit bull loose down the street."

You gaze over in the direction he's pointing and sure enough, there is a pit bull without a collar, devouring an alley cat and barking wildly at cars passing by. Wow, that guy may have just saved you from getting mauled to death like that cat!

Then you notice the homeless man has a cup with "homeless and hungry" scribbled on it with a crayon. Are you now more interested in dropping a buck or two in there? The answer (if you're a human being, which I think you are) is yes. We don't mind being interrupted if it helps us, and we are much more likely to give to people who give to us first. It's basic reciprocity, and it's wired deep into our DNA. This is how marketing works.

Lead Generation Tip #4. Treat "Money Pages" Carefully

Some of your pages should focus on the content first and the opt-in second. If a post is driving serious conversions, you want to keep readers on the page for as long as possible. Consider sticking to exit intent pop-ups for pages that sell products well. If you have a review post that converts visitors into buyers at a high rate, don't interrupt their reading process. Wait until they are about to leave the page and then show them an opt-in. As I mentioned already, any good lead capture software will have this sort of functionality.

Lead Generation Tip #5. Don't Show Opt-Ins to Existing Subscribers

There are many tools that can help us prevent email subscribers from seeing pop-ups to things they've already opted into. The last thing we want to do is annoy readers by showing them things they already received!

Lead Generation Tip #6. Test Display on Mobile Devices

I made the huge mistake of not cross-checking an early lead magnet pop-up on mobile and tablet. I was annoying my visitors AND they couldn't even opt-in because of a formatting error.

Chapter Summary

- Email (or something very similar) will be the greatest source of owned traffic for the foreseeable future.
- If you have a website (you should), be aggressive and remember that most visitors won't ever come back. You

rarely get multiple chances to get someone onto your owned traffic list, so use your chance wisely.

- Never stop testing your opt-ins and they will never stop improving.
- Offset any pop-up annoyance by providing abnormally high value with your opt-ins.

Analyzing Affiliate Offers

There are a limitless number of potential merchant offers across every single niche imaginable. The shiny lure of these can lead you toward one of the big mistakes most affiliate marketers make: promoting too many things at the same time.

When I first started affiliate marketing, I adopted a "more is more" mentality. I assumed that the more affiliate offers I promoted, the more money I'd make. That was dead wrong. Here's why.

First, forgive me if this sounds dramatic, we're all cursed with the limitation of time. Obviously, I knew this, but I assumed it was okay since it doesn't take long to sign up for these programs. I would just casually plug them into content and promotions when I can. This just doesn't work as well in practice as it sounds on paper. A spray-and-pray approach doesn't lead to a sizeable amount of sales spread thin and wide across all the programs; it leads to little to no sales across all the programs.

If the affiliate product you're promoting is so good that just a casual mention drives big sales, it's highly likely you're promoting something extremely competitive and many people will already use it and won't be in the market to actually buy from you.

If the products aren't competitive, they'll require more than a onetime promotion. They'll require focus and multiple "touch points." This goes back to the marketing "Rule of Seven," which states that on average, customers need to see a product at least seven times before they buy. Every year it seems this number increases and is more like the Rule of Ten to Twenty thanks to the increased amount of competition and other shiny objects pulling for our potential customer's attention.

So what do we need to do? It's perfectly fine to register for as many affiliate programs as you'd like, but it's critical that you give focused effort to a handful that are proven to be winners. But what makes a winning affiliate program? It goes far beyond whether it makes commissions for you (although that's paramount of course).

When choosing which affiliate programs to enter long-term, focused relationships with, you need to ask the following questions.

1. Is the Product High Quality?

I wish this went without saying, but the products you promote need to make you look fantastic. If your audience discovers that you're promoting subpar products because they make you more money, you won't last long. The products should be the genuinely best option available to solve whatever needs your customers have. This extends to things like customer support and brand presence. The products you promote will reflect on you.

Here's a hard truth: if there's a free option that is better than the paid option, promote the free one if you want to maintain a long-term relationship of trust with your customers. Remember, trust sells. You build trust (and therefore future sales) by sacrificing some sales along the way.

Your personal experience is definitely the best way to judge quality, but it isn't the end-all. It has shocked me when I've found out that my referrals did not receive the same experience from vendors that I did."

2. Does the Vendor Support Their Affiliates?

Not all affiliate programs are created equal. It's incredible how much more effort some companies put into their affiliate programs than others. This goes well beyond how much they pay. A great affiliate program should want their affiliates to succeed because that means they will succeed. They put in the extra work needed to help their affilaites help them. Several affiliate programs I've been a part of have an opposite dynamic. They seem to want the referrals but don't put in the work to support their affiliates to drive more of them.

3. Is There a Robust Affiliate Dashboard with Swipe Copy, Assets, and Alternate Incoming Links?

If the vendor really supports their affiliates, they will show that in their dashboards. One feature I find valuable is the ability to create alternate incoming links. These are links that direct visitors to different pages on the vendor's site while giving you an affiliate cookie. Many of the products and services I promote have their own blog content, and the ability to create alternate incoming links allows me to send traffic to non-sales pages while also warming up my audience to the product and potentially making sales.

For example, I can take a merchant's blog post URL and append my cookie to it. This means that whenever someone clicks the link to read the post, I get paid if they buy! This is much classier than just plugging a direct link to the sales pages. Most of the great affiliate programs have this functionality. If you haven't looked, check it out.

I love to take content from my affiliates and create email broadcasts around it and plug them into automations. This provides a steady stream of new clicks that will slowly convert into new referrals.

Also, sometimes you might want to send traffic straight to the checkout page. More rudimentary affiliate programs provide just one link, and it typically directs to the home page. Having alternate incoming links allows you to send traffic straight to the checkout page if you'd like. Keep in mind, this isn't always the best approach, but it's good to have the ability to do it when appropriate.

4. Is There a Dedicated Affiliate Manager?
Affiliate managers often get paid a percentage of total affiliate sales, so a great manager will help you along the way to make sales.

5. Are There Regular Incentives, Contests, and Promotions?
My favorite affiliate programs regularly run contests and promotions that reward their top affiliates.

6. Do You Trust That They Track Sales Properly?
I wish this wasn't an issue, but many affiliate programs simply don't attribute sales properly. You can see this for yourself when an affiliate offers their products across multiple networks and the metrics are wildly different. This is often a result of flawed software, but there are also bad actors who will do everything possible to remove affiliate attribution at every chance possible.

7. Do They Offer Exclusive, Customized Deals and Coupon Codes?
All of my top affiliate programs have provided me with a customized coupon code. These not only help with conversions (with some odd exceptions) but they also add an extra layer of security that you'll receive credit for sales since codes usually override cookies. If someone is browsing with a cookie blocker, you can still get attribution with a code.

A code also allows you to promote via audio or video without sharing links. One thing to be aware of is whether the company is providing you with a deal that is equal to the others on the market. I've seen many affiliates offer their own deals that are far better than what they give affiliates. That is their right, but it makes it more difficult to make sales if that code overrides affiliate attribution even if you were the first to make the customer aware of the product.

Also, a great affiliate program is likely willing to help you get a custom landing page created for your offer. This is a special version of the vendor's sales page that is customized to show your affiliation. It can include things like your company logo, images of you and phrases like "partnered with," or "special offers for followers of. . . ."

I've found that most well-managed affiliate programs are more than happy to help their affiliates boost conversions by creating a customized landing page for them. It's a win-win and doesn't take them a lot of effort to complete.

Only about 1/10 of the products I promote do this for their affiliates, but the increase in conversion rates is noticeable and well worth it.

8. Does the Affiliate Program Retarget Traffic You Send Them?

Many of the best affiliate programs put in the work after you send them traffic to make a sale. They pixel their traffic and spend their own money to run ads to remind customers to buy. This is hugely beneficial to you as an affiliate marketer. That is, of course, assuming they still attribute commissions on retargeting conversions.

9. Do They Have a Sales Funnel and Is It Valuable?

Great companies know the value of sales funnels. If you promote a product that has a sales funnel in place, your EPC (earnings per click) is going to get much higher. Make sure that you're getting commissions on the upsells, but that is a pretty standard practice.

Be careful though; sometimes the sales funnel is a deterrent for me. For example, let's say that I'm promoting product X that is something I know is high quality and a great fit for my audience. However, whenever someone buys product X, they get thrown into one of those "you can always find someone who will pay too much" sales funnels. They're now exposed to products that I might not actually recommend and it looks like I support them because of my initial endorsement that got them there.

10. Is the Payout Fair?

Payout shouldn't limit what you promote, but it certainly should be a part of deciding what affiliate programs to spend more time on.

We promote the best products regardless of payout, but we focus on the best products that also have the best payouts.

11. Does the Program Have Opportune and Fair Terms and Conditions?

We need to be crystal clear on the terms of whatever products we promote.

- Can we run paid traffic? If so, are there limitations such as no brand names?
- Is there a minimum number of sales before payout or deactivation?
- What is the attribution style? First click and last click are both used, but most affiliates I've surveyed favor last click. Just be aware of what the attribution is.
- What are the cookie durations?

Understanding the terms and conditions is critical. Be vigilant to notice any changes to these because many programs change very often.

Chapter Summary

- Not all affiliate programs are created equal. Avoid spending too much effort with affiliate programs that aren't high quality.
- If a product serves your audience, you shouldn't avoid mentioning it just because the affiliate program isn't amazing. However, you shouldn't dedicate too much time to marketing campaigns for poor programs.

CORE CONCEPTS AND MINDSET

Give More than You Take

Marketers walk a fine line between giving and taking. Far too often marketers jump straight into sales mode before they've done a single thing to actually build the trust of their new follower. You see this in email sequences that are basically month-long sales pitches or in the blog pop-ups that shove a high ticket paid product down the throat of every person who visits their page.

Highlight this: Stop trying to get paid for everything you do. In the data-driven world of digital marketing, everyone seems to focus on the next sale. They want things they can quantify and, unfortunately, goodwill isn't something we can pin a number on. However, it's a critical part of making sales as an affiliate marketer. We discussed earlier that trust is an enormous factor in conversion rates, and trust is built or destroyed by how much we give versus how much we take (sell).

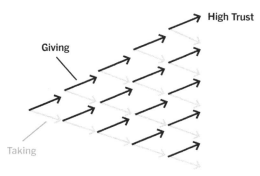

The rule of thumb: always over-deliver. Give away things for free that others are charging for. Build goodwill relentlessly and it will show through in your conversion rates when it is time to actually sell something.

Basic human psychology is on your side when it comes to giving more than you take. We are wired to want to give back to those who have given to us. This is known as the social norm of reciprocity. Reciprocity means that in response to friendly actions, people are frequently much nicer and much more cooperative than predicted by the self-interest model; conversely, in response to hostile actions they are frequently much more nasty and even brutal.[4]

Phillip Kunz demonstrated the power of the automatic nature of reciprocity in 1976 when he conducted an experiment with Christmas cards. In his experiment, Kunz sent out holiday cards with pictures of his family and a short note to total strangers. To his surprise, many holiday cards came flooding back to him from these people whom he had never met.[5] Most of these replies didn't ask about Kunz or why he was sending cards in the first place. It was merely a common reaction to give back once someone has given to us.

This works both ways. If you negatively impact someone, they will be more likely to do something negative to you. If you sell someone a scammy product, for example, they will be far more likely to speak ill of you whenever your name is brought up.

---

4 Ernst Fehr and Simon Gächter, "Fairness and Retaliation: The Economics of Reciprocity," *Journal of Economic Perspectives* 14, no. 3 (Summer 2000): 159–81, https://www.aeaweb.org/articles?id=10.1257/jep.14.3.159.
5 Philip R. Kunz and Michael Woolcott, "Season's Greetings: From My Status to Yours," *Social Science Research* 5, no. 3 (September 1976): 269–78, https://www.sciencedirect.com/science/article/abs/pii/0049089X7690003X?via%3Dihub.

Chapter Summary

- Effective affiliate marketing requires giving more than you take. When in doubt, give more value away for free than you think you should.
- Selling too often without providing consistent value will cause your followers to lose trust in you and damage your overall chances of turning them into customers.

Large Audiences Hide Bad Marketing

This book is going to teach you the things that will help you maximize your affiliate earnings regardless of how large your following is. Most of you will not have large followings at the time that you're reading this book, and that is perfectly fine. However, you deserve to know the truth.

It's no secret that a large audience makes earning money as an affiliate marketer much easier. Most of the people who get rich through affiliate marketing aren't amazing at the art of affiliate marketing. The nuances like testing, writing high-converting copy, and mastering paid traffic channels is not their priority. But somehow, it still works. They make sales because they've built large followings. People follow them because they're attractive, funny, charismatic, or smart.

With consistency, many people build a gold mine of attention and often don't even realize that they're sitting on a gold mine of opportunity. They become so involved and engaged with creating a connection with their followers that they haven't even thought about getting paid for it.

They can easily monetize when they choose to, and it isn't nearly as difficult for them as it is for a new aspiring marketer with no reach. Their followers know, like, and/or trust them (usually all three), and when they have something to sell, it's pretty simple.

It's a numbers game. If they promote a product that fits their audience and converts reasonably well on its own, they can start cashing checks whenever they want. They have the luxury of saying, "Hey, here's this, it's cool, buy it," and they can create what I call "revenue events" fast.

Big Audience vs. Small Audience

100,000 Clicks *3% CR = 3,000 Sales

Larger Audience with lower Conversion Rates
Smaller Audience with Higher Conversion Rates

10,000 Clicks *6% CR = 600 Sales

People with large audiences don't need to be as tactical as those of us with smaller audiences need to be. They can take low conversion rates and make up for it at scale. A massive audience can hide a lot of mistakes and make it far less important to focus as much on some of the more granular tactics you're about to learn.

Most influencers eventually get help with maximizing their sales and conversions by hiring people like me who know how to get more out of each follower. They can afford it, and the cycle continues. The rich get richer.

This can dishearten new affiliate marketers because growing a large audience is difficult. I'm also not a believer that everyone is cut out for the spotlight of having a huge audience. It's not for everyone.

However, I need you to understand that growing an audience is the key to unlocking your maximum earning potential as an affiliate marketer. I highly recommend that everyone works to grow their reach if they want to become the wealthiest affiliate marketer in their space.

You may think, "Why should I even bother with affiliate marketing until I have an enormous amount of followers?" or, "I don't want to be an influencer with a huge audience; why bother with affiliate marketing at all?"

Now, growing a following and getting lots of free traffic is extremely valuable, and I recommend trying to capitalize on that if you want to. But this book will not require you to do that. Do you have 1,000,000 subscribers on YouTube? This is for you. Do you have 100 members in a Facebook group? This is for you as well. Have no followers at all? That's totally fine too—it's actually a nice place to be since you probably don't have any bad habits yet. This book will lay a strong foundation for you for growth.

Yes, we will cover ways to grow your following. But I want to give you the cold, hard tactics that will help you get the most out of any size audience as quickly as possible.

Chapter Summary

- It's not a secret that having a large audience makes earning big commissions easier.
- If you're cut out for it, continually grow your audience and your sales will never stop increasing.
- You can still be a highly successful affiliate marketer without a large audience; you will just need to be very effective in your strategies and execution.

Almost Nothing Works

"I have not failed. I've just found 10,000 ways that won't work."

Thomas A. Edison

What a bummer of a concept, right? Well bear with me because without accepting this bitter truth you'll never give yourself a real chance to see results.

Most of what you do as an affiliate marketer early on will fail. The odds of launching a campaign or promotion and it immediately catching on are extremely slim. This isn't just to be accepted, it is to be expected.

Most things fail. Winning is carried by the few massive successes

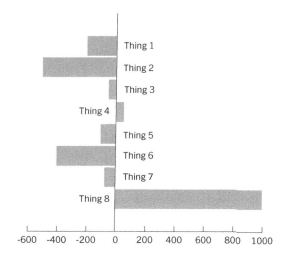

Don't get me wrong, I've never been a fan of brushing off failures like they're a positive thing. The "fail forward" mantra means well and has surely helped many people, but it's over-romanticized. There are an infinite number of ways to fail. By comparison, there are marginally fewer ways to succeed.

It's like throwing a dart at a dartboard and assuming that since you missed ten inches low, you'll know not to miss ten inches low again. You adjust and work to raise your throw a bit, but it's still much more of a numbers game or resilience. The bullseye is a tiny bit of area compared to the vast area around it that you could hit with your throw. Once you find a rhythm, you will hit the bullseye more frequently. Successful marketing is about finding that rhythm and getting your throws in.

You don't need everything to work. You need to take a massive amount of action and the smaller number of efforts that become successful can more than make up for what might have initially seemed like lost time. Most efforts fail, so we need to increase our chances by putting in more of them.

As you grow as an affiliate marketer, you'll have more of a safety net. You'll have more experience, hopefully a sizable amount of owned traffic to test with, and more capital and time to spend tinkering around without the fear of not being able to pay your bills.

Most people fail at affiliate marketing, and it's because they see their first failures as failures of the entire process as opposed to an inevitable part of the process. Failure is part of the process; let the process play out. Keep learning, testing, and adapting. The successes will wash out the failures if you're resilient enough to stick around long enough to reach them.

I can't tell you that you will succeed quickly, but I do believe that anyone who doesn't give up will always find success with affiliate marketing eventually. Do you have what it takes to stay the course? Never give up and your success is inevitable.

Chapter Summary

- Failure is not just inevitable, it is part of the process.
- Success doesn't come overnight. Most of the things you do will either not work or will not show results for longer than you expected.
- You will always win with affiliate marketing as long as you don't give up.

Your Cornerstone Product

In a later chapter, we're going to go over choosing the best affiliate programs, but first I want to explain an important concept. The most successful affiliate marketers I know make most of their commissions from a single affiliate offer. I call these offers "cornerstone products."

No matter what niche you're in, you should be able to find one of these types of products. These products will be the bedrock of your business. Anyone who follows you should see this product at least once.

On a website, they will see it on the banners and relevantly placed throughout your content. In a video they will see a link in the description. In your email newsletter they will get at least one dedicated email promoting the product. It will be the lifeblood of your business.

Great cornerstone products should meet the following criteria:

Cornerstone Criteria #1. Be a "Must Have" or Obvious First Purchase for Your Reader

The term "cornerstone" applies not just to you but also to the reader. A perfect cornerstone offer will be something that everyone in your space needs.

Many of the things that affiliate marketers promote are just "nice to have." Things that are great if you have money to spend and can use them, but not mandatory to remain in the space.

If your audience is internet entrepreneurs who build websites, they all need hosting. Hosting is the cornerstone for them, and it's not optional if they want a true online presence. If someone doesn't have hosting, they won't be in your target audience for long. They will be window shoppers as opposed to serious buyers and action takers. You're doing them a tremendous favor by helping them make a wise decision right out of the gate.

This doesn't mean that your audience is now limited to newbies in your space since you will make a majority of your sales from an introductory offer. Many people who find your content will already have the product you're offering or an alternative. That is to be expected.

If a "must have" product doesn't seem to exist, your cornerstone product should be something that a majority of your audience would want to have as soon as possible. For example, in the gaming space you could promote your favorite headset. These aren't absolutely mandatory, but they are pretty close to it, and they might become more appealing over time to all of your followers.

Cornerstone Criteria #2. Be Reasonably Priced

"Reasonably priced" is a relative term. Going back to the hosting example, there are different price points ranging from a few bucks a month to thousands of dollars per year or more.

The difference between the lowest priced hosting services and the highest priced hosting services is noticeable only at scale. People new to the space who are just trying to get their first website online don't need many of the higher-end features like extended storage space. Therefore, the best cornerstone hosting would be the lower-cost plans. If the product has tiers that go into the higher end, that is perfectly fine, but your core offer should be the entry-level price points.

Cornerstone Criteria #3. Be an Amazing Product

Great affiliate marketers know they can make a lot more money by selling repeatedly to the same people. They don't promote off-quality products just to get quick and easy sales because they understand that trust is extremely valuable. If the first product you promote is a total waste of money, don't expect the buyer to ever trust you again. If it wows them, you could have a loyal follower for life. (We cover what makes a great affiliate product and affiliate program in more detail in a later chapter.)

Cornerstone Criteria #4. Recurring Commission (Bonus)

This isn't mandatory, but the cornerstone product is very often something that can drive recurring revenue. Since it's a cornerstone product (something the buyer has to have) you can continue getting paid for it as long as they are an active member of the space.

If possible, look for a software to promote. Those are more often than not recurring subscriptions and have always performed best for me. Don't force this if there isn't a viable recurring product option in your space, but keep this in mind as you're looking into all the options.

Here are some examples of perfect cornerstone products.

- You teach people how to make their gyms more profitable, so you promote a subscription gym management software.
- You teach people how to save money on their taxes, so you recommend your favorite bookkeeping software.

Here are some examples of pretty good cornerstone products if you can't find a perfect one.

- You're an influencer in the homeschooling space, so you promote a line of textbooks you love.
- You're an influencer in the fitness space, so you promote a supplement membership.
- You have a vlog about food allergies and recommend an at-home food allergy testing kit. As an added benefit, there's a membership option that gives them a discount on new kits each month.

Ask yourself this question: If I had to promote a product at the beginning or end of every piece of content I produce, what would it be? That should be your cornerstone product.

Chapter Summary

- All affiliate marketers should have one cornerstone product.
- A great cornerstone product should be something that most of your audience has to have, is reasonably priced, and is high quality.
- Recurring commission products are ideal for cornerstone products since they are things the buyer will use as long as they're in the niche, but this isn't mandatory.

Golden Rules of Email Marketing

Email marketing is one of the evergreen tactics that isn't going anywhere soon. It's so important that if I waited to cover it in any section besides this first one, it would be a disservice to my readers. It is another topic that deserves an entire book and ongoing testing and real-world application to truly learn everything you would want to know. For this book, I've trimmed this down into the most valuable rules of email marketing. Follow these and you'll outperform most of the people in your niche.

Rule #1 Give Tremendous Value
Rule #2 Protect Your Sender Reputation
Rule #3 Prune Inactive Subscribers
Rule #4 Remain Consistent
Rule #5 Tag and Segment
Rule #6 Spend More Time in the Subject Line
Rule #7 Test Continually and Review the Data
Rule #8 Find an Automations Balance
Rule #9 Focus on Readability and Get to the Point Quickly
Rule #10 Be Personal, Not Commerical

Rule 1. Give Tremendous Value
If your emails to your mailing list are just long-winded, never-ending sales pitches, your open rates and click through rates will

underachieve. Give your readers a reason to open your emails by regularly providing extreme value in whatever way possible. Get creative, and remember that value is fuel for future revenue.

Rule 2. Protect Your Sender Reputation

Play by the rules, no matter how stringent they may be. Bad actors have been abusing email marketing for decades, and all of us are paying the price for it. Email service providers are trigger-happy with marking senders as malicious once enough subscribers have reported their broadcasts as spam or worthy of the junk folder. If you break rules such as contacting email subscribers who didn't opt-in to your list, you will pay a permanent price.

One of the best ways to burn your sender reputation is to send misleading subject lines. Never pretend an email is something that it isn't. Yes, your open rates will be great, but you will risk enraging your subscribers, losing trust, and being reported as spam. Here are some examples of what some marketers try to pull off.

- Adding "RE:" or "FWD:" to a subject line to make it appear that you're in an existing conversation rather than a general broadcast.
- Creating false fear with subjects such as, "Warning: Account at Risk" or "Your card couldn't be processed" when there was no actual issue.
- Flat out lying with false promises such as "You've won" when there was no actual contest.

If the subject doesn't match with the email, don't send it. It's as simple as that. Subscribers who were tricked into clicking aren't valuable clicks, and you damage the chances of them ever being valuable in the future.

Rule 3. Prune Inactive Subscribers

This goes along with protecting your sender reputation. If you have subscribers who never open your emails, email service providers will associate your account with being low value or, even worse, as a spammer. This means ripping off the Band-aid from time to time. I recommend you quarterly create re-engagement sequences and remove subscribers who do not engage with your broadcasts. It may seem counterintuitive, but more is not more in the world of email marketing.

Rule 4. Remain Consistent

The biggest mistake I see marketers make is that they don't contact their list often enough. Although this is less annoying than contacting your list too often with nonsense, there is a healthy middle ground. If you have well-targeted segments and you're creating great emails, feel confident sending broadcasts at a minimum of once a week. My sweet spot is one or two broadcasts to each subscriber per week. If your niche responds well to more than that, by all means, send more.

The best email lists that I'm on send their broadcasts out around the same time on the same day of each week. This is an awesome way to keep your subscribers on the lookout for your emails and to get in the habit of opening them since they won't be surprised. Find the optimal time through testing and focus on sending more emails during those time frames.

Rule 5. Tag and Segment

Quality email marketing requires quality list segmentation. Although I'm a huge believer in the idea that less is usually more, list segmenting is an exception. You should do more when it comes to segmentation.

If you don't tag your email subscribers properly, you'll never truly reach your full earning potential with email marketing. You'll continually send emails to people who don't want them and miss out on sending emails to the people who do. Failing to properly tag your subscribers leads to unnecessary unsubscribes, lost sales, and a damaged reputation to boot.

Putting proper systems into place may seem like a daunting and complex task at first, but trust me, it's well worth the time and effort up front. That is, of course, if you really want to make email marketing work for your business. Which you do, right?

So what are email tags? Tags are the fundamental form of list segmentation. They're attributions assigned to specific emails on our mailing list that let us know more about who a subscriber is. Things like what they've purchased, what they're interested in, or what caused them to join the mailing list in the first place.

Proper tags allow us to do the following:

- reduce unsubscribes
- reduce complaints
- better understand our subscribers
- increase click through rates
- increase conversion rates
- improve overall deliverability
- improve our relationships with our subscribers

Although you can get away with poor segmentation early in your career when your list is small, as your list grows and the number of ways you collect leads diversifies, you'll be in serious trouble if you don't tag properly.

If you haven't been tagging your subscribers, it's okay. It's not too late to start. In a later chapter I'll go into more detail about the tags I recommend you use.

Rule 6. Spend More Time on the Subject Line

"On the average, five times as many people read the headline as read the body copy. When you have written your headline, you have spent eighty cents out of your dollar."

—David Ogilvy

Your email subject lines are the same as a headline on an article or advertisement. Your writing process should always start with the subject line and write everything else after. Get in the habit of writing several subject lines and then narrowing the results down. This is an exercise you must perform every time you write an email if you want to maximize the value of your list.

A/B TEST RESULTS

A esrever sourcing			B [video] esrever sourcing		
1576	**23.7%**	**1.8%**	**1576**	**21.3%**	**1.8%**
RECIPIENTS	OPEN RATE	CLICK RATE	RECIPIENTS	OPEN RATE	CLICK RATE

Rule 7. Test Continually and Review the Data

Every good email marketing software will allow you to run A/B tests of at least the subject lines. Some allow you to test further elements in the body of the email, but at the very least, you should run an A/B test for each email you send.

If an email works particularly well, copy the style again in the future. If a broadcast email does well, I always consider whether I can add it to an automation that is sent to future subscribers during their onboarding.

Rule 8. Find an Automations Balance

There is no better time to contact a subscriber than immediately after they've subscribed. If you wait too long, they may no longer be interested in the product or topic, or they may not recognize you or remember subscribing. This leads to a lot of unnecessary spam complaints. "Who the heck is this? I never opted in to this." (Clicks report as spam).

Use the tools of automation available to you and send email sequences that provide your new subscribers with tremendous value while introducing them to you and your brand. A good automation sequence should do any or all of the following:

- Introduce yourself and your brand.
- Invite the new subscriber to reply to your email (this will dramatically increase the chances of them being white labeled and receiving all future broadcasts you send).
- Encourage them to follow you on other mediums.
- Introduce them to your cornerstone affiliate product.
- Send them to your best content.
- Further tag and segment them based on what actions they take.

How long an email sequence should be is up for debate. Personally, I don't like to go further than two weeks out at a time. I send far more emails in the first two weeks than I will going forward.

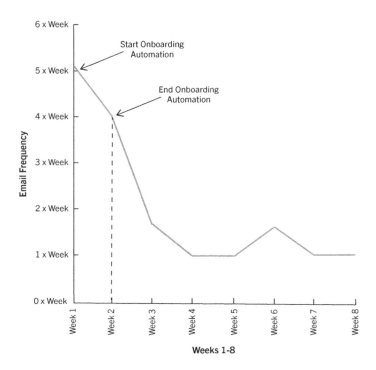

The illustration above shows what my average email sequence frequency looks like for a new subscriber. This does two things. It helps prune people who don't really want my emails, and it gets me optimal exposure when the subscriber is still "hot" for the topic or products I promote.

One exception that I make is that I send several emails if a promotion is about to end. We will cover this more in the chapter titled Beat the Buzzer.

Rule 9. Focus on Readability and Get to the Point Quickly

Your broadcasts only need to be as long as necessary to optimize clicks and no longer. Make every email easy to skim on both mobile and desktop browsers. This means using bullet points, making calls to action clear, and providing enough white space in the email to make it easy on the eyes. Also, although I like the look of dark backgrounds and lighter colored text, studies show that having dark text and light backgrounds dramatically improves the readability of your content.

Also, use the pre-header text space if possible. This is the preview content that appears under the subject line. This will allow you to convey your message to your subscribers even if they don't open the email. It's also an additional way to drive clicks since you can add extra copy to pique the subscriber's interest.

Pre-Header Text Examples

Rule 10. Be Personal, Not Commercial

Your newsletter is a chance for you to build your relationship with your subscribers. Avoid looking like a car dealership that is running their "whatever-a-thon" promotion. You know the emails I'm talking about. Tons of sales graphics, flashing banners, and bright colors. Not only are these impersonal, they are also magnets for the "promotions" or junk folders of the subscriber's inbox. Leave that style for the used car salespeople. You focus on writing emails as if they were being sent directly to a friend.

Chapter Summary

- Email marketing is a critical, evergreen part of affiliate marketing.
- Mastering email marketing takes practice and ongoing effort, but the ten rules outlined in this chapter will give you a majority of what you need to know.

CONTENT CREATION

The Six Content Purposes

"Definiteness of purpose is the starting point of all achievement."

—W. Clement Stone

Part of the reason many people fail with content marketing is that they blindly create and rarely pause to ask why they're creating at all.

What will this blog post do for you and your readers? Why is this video worth watching and worth your time?

Get into the habit of having a definiteness of purpose before you create any piece of content and your path to success will become much more linear. Although much of the content you create won't pan out like you hoped, the overall trajectory of your content marketing will be much more consistent.

In talking about "purpose," I've broken it down into six core types. They cover everything that content marketers value, and if you're making content without knowing which type it is, it will not be as effective.

Purpose #1. Organic Traffic Bait

Organic traffic bait posts are focused on attracting relevant, organic visits through search engines. Primarily Google and primarily in the native region of the website, but traffic outside of these demographics is more than welcome.

These posts have the potential to rank highly on Google and receive a lot of clicks from multiple semantic keywords. Although it's fantastic to rank for higher-difficulty terms, it's quicker and easier to rank for keywords with low competition. Every niche is flooded with blog post topics that could almost immediately drive organic traffic.

Purpose #2. Super Fan Builder

This sort of content is extremely valuable but is unlikely to drive a large amount of organic traffic. It solves an exact problem for fewer people, but they will love you for it. These sorts of articles are perfect for sending to your owned traffic sources such as your mailing list or your social media channels.

The goal here isn't to make any money or go viral. The goal is to take a small segment of my followers and turn them into huge fans. This concept is outlined brilliantly by Kevin Kelly in his classic blog post "1,000 True Fans."

> "To be a successful creator you don't need millions. You don't need millions of dollars or millions of customers, millions of clients or millions of fans. To make a living as a craftsperson, photographer, musician, designer, author, animator, app maker, entrepreneur, or inventor you need only thousands of true fans."[6]

Kelly goes on to explain that if you can get 1,000 people who are big enough fans of your work that they will spend just $100/year with you, you can easily make $100,000/year. For whatever rea-

---

6   Kevin Kelly, "1,000 True Fans," The Technium, March 4, 2008, https://kk.org/thetechnium/1000-true-fans.

son, this is the number that internet entrepreneurs seem to glorify as the "I've made it" amount of money.

Creating content that doesn't sell but makes your readers become bigger fans of your work will pay off. The richest affiliate marketers know that they get paid from super fan builder content, they just don't see the money directly and immediately. It's the most lucrative long-term play any marketer can make.

Purpose #3. Share Bait

These are pieces that can get large amounts of traffic but through social sharing rather than search engines. These posts are things that are unique, creative, timely, or extremely interesting that others want to be first to share. They are things that people would love to read but might not have ever typed into a search engine.

This is like when you're introduced to a new song. You didn't know exactly how to find it, but somehow it landed in front of you and you love it. If you're like most people, you'll want to share it with others.

It can be easier to create this sort of content with video and audio mediums since they rely less on search intent and people are used to stumbling upon great content rather than actively pursuing it.

Creating share-worthy content takes practice. For inspiration, regularly check out sites like BuzzFeed.com and Lifehacker.com to see how they do it. They are the gold standards of share-worthy content. (We will cover this in more detail in the chapter "Curation = Creation.")

Purpose #4. Backlink Bait

Backlinks are links from other websites to your website. It shows search engines that other sites believe you're credible enough to be cited as a source, and that makes the search engine trust you more.

More trust from search engines means that it's easier for you to rank for key search terms.

As much as I hope search engines find better ways to identify what content is worth ranking first, backlinks seem like they're here to stay. This means we have to be deliberate with creating content that attracts them.

Some articles are much more likely to attract backlinks because they contain some unique data or takeaway. These help boost the entire blog by building domain authority.

Here are some characteristics that make a post more likely to get backlinks:

- easy to cite
- contains research or data
- unique (preferably)
- interesting
- ranks at the top of search engines

One post like this that drives a massive amount of high-quality backlinks can catapult your blog's authority, which will have a ripple effect that will improve your rankings across all of your content.

Purpose #5. Buyer Intent Bait

These are pieces of content that target hot traffic that is ready to buy. A majority of your sales will come from these posts. These posts include words like:

- "review"
- "comparison"
- "alternative to"
- "discount"

- "coupon code"
- "free trial"

Anything that signals someone is ready to buy or is strongly considering buying something is considered high buyer intent. Although these are the "bread and butter" for earnings, they can be difficult to rank because it's hard to get anyone to link to your clearly monetized content. These pieces are hard to rank, but there is gold at the end of the rainbow if you can.

Purpose #6. Engagement Bait

This is the most abstract form of content we can create, and it typically comes in the form of email broadcasts or social media posts. I also refer to these as "top-of-mind bumps" since the main goal is to make sure your brand stays atop the minds of your audience. Although this sounds somewhat pitiful, remember, we live in a world full of thousands of companies constantly vying for the attention of our followers. When done correctly, engagement bait is fun and effective.

I'm not a believer that "all press is good press," or in this case "all attention is good attention." This might work in politics or music, but it doesn't fit well with affiliate marketing. Stirring negative attention can cause you to lose the trust of your audience, which will then cost you potential sales. Don't be afraid to be yourself, but be careful to protect your brand image. Avoid appearing desperate for attention at all costs.

There is more to content purposes than may meet the eye. First, understand that content can have multiple purposes. One post can fit more than one purpose, and some articles do indeed accomplish all six (although they are unicorns). If you can make a piece of content accomplish multiple goals, then by all means do so as long as it doesn't dampen the overall impact of the content.

Sometimes, focusing on just one type of purpose will be optimal.

Finally, make sure that all content has some sort of call to action. With few exceptions, you should always try to turn traffic into followers on other owned platforms. This means including relevant calls to action for visitors to join your mailing list, subscribe to your channel, or follow you across other social networks.

Sometimes the traffic you're driving isn't a fit for an owned audience. For example, if I write blog posts that simply syndicate the latest funny memes, collecting emails is not likely worth the cost of the subscriber. If I'm intent on creating this sort of content, I will need to make sure that I can get them to click on a display ad or some other form of on-page monetization. Without that, I am not getting paid to create and I'm not growing my brand. That is fine, of course, if that's what you want, but I doubt that's why you're reading this book.

Chapter Summary

- Everything we create should serve an intentional purpose.
- Balance the types of content purposes you use. Too much buyer intent content, for example, will hurt your credibility and long-term sales.
- The six core content purposes are: organic traffic bait, super fan builder, share bait, backlink bait, buyer intent bait, and engagement bait (or top-of-mind bumps).

Measure Twice, Cut Once

The early adopters to the internet marketing space had the first mover advantage, but they missed out on something that we have now that makes our work much easier. Data and nearly limitless access to it.

We can make better decisions on what will work and what won't thanks to the rabbit trails left by others who have done the work before us. Even better, we have a nearly endless array of tools to use to quickly analyze and make sense of it all. This means that we don't have to start from scratch every time we try something new. This applies to many different things.

- Research what people are looking for on search engines before writing a blog post or filming a video.
- Research what sorts of ads your competitors are running before spending too much of your own money.
- Research what topics are trending and jump on them early.
- Research seasonal trends in buyer behavior and remember to capitalize on them when they come back around.

While there is more than enough room for spontaneity and being the first to try something, in most cases, data will help make better decisions. Decisions that will help you get results faster, more easily, and while spending less money.

The key is remembering to use data when possible. When I started creating content online, I didn't do any kind of research. This wasn't a terrible thing since it kept me interested and passionate about the things I wrote about. However, it did slow the growth of organic traffic I received.

Although my content was fun to write, it wasn't fun knowing that there was no one reading it. I essentially had a virtual diary that was only being read by me when I proofread my content. Had I used the tools at my disposal, I could have chosen topics better. Topics that people were dying to see covered and that would have driven floods of traffic to my site long before it had very much authority.

My mistake was spending too much time creating content and not enough time on the research. You can grow exponentially faster than I did if you remember to "measure twice and cut once." Creating a fraction of the content but with better research will almost always outperform the "spray and pray" approach. Don't wing it. You simply don't have enough time to waste.

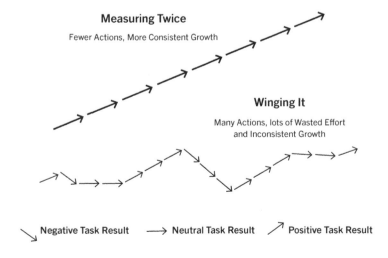

Now this doesn't mean that you should only chase after easy traffic or that everything you write needs to be catered to data. As your brand grows and you build up your owned traffic, you can start to write those passion topics and know that you'll get readers immediately, without the help of any search engines or social media platforms.

Chapter Summary

- Doing deep research before creating content can save you a tremendous amount of time, money, and effort.

Skyscraper Approach: How to Stand on the (Content) Shoulders of Giants

Competition isn't a bad thing. In fact, competition can help us create better content because we can compare our work to what others have already made.

We use something called the "Skyscraper Approach," which means we make our content better than the best content on the topic. Imagine a skyscraper that is twenty stories high; in this analogy we would want our skyscraper to be twenty-one stories high. The "height" is a metaphor for content value, and there are many ways we can make our content better (taller) than the existing content on the topic.

Skyscraper Approach

Your Content   The Next Best Content

For instance, if you write a post titled "Athletic Greens Review," you would have (at the time of this writing) over a dozen other articles to compare your article against. Focus on pages in the top spots on the given platform and check out:

- content length
- images
- title
- headings
- SEO

If I make a post, I want it to always be the best on the topic (until someone skyscrapers me of course). This doesn't guarantee that you'll outrank these other pages, but you'll dramatically improve your brand reputation and overall traffic over time by creating grade-A content.

The skyscraper approach is primarily mentioned in SEO circles, but it can be used in any of the three mediums (audio, video, or writing). Leverage the content of your competitors and know that they will be doing the same to you.

This approach of analyzing the best content on a topic goes deeper than just basic SEO and outranking our competitors. This is also a mindset that all affiliate marketers need to adopt. We need to immerse ourselves in the relevant work around us.

The best content creators are often the most voracious consumers of content on their topic. To truly unleash your potential to create amazing content, you need to surround yourself with amazing content from the leaders in your space and the tertiary spaces that have some relevant overlap.

The 2:1 consume-to-create ratio means that for every unit of time spent creating information or fact-based content, spend an equal or greater amount of time consuming content around that topic.

2:1 Consume to Create

2 x Researching   **1 x Creating**

Even though I've consumed more information about affiliate marketing than most people ever will in their lifetime, I still spent time to read the top ten on affiliate marketing that I could find while writing this book. Why? I want my book to be the best. How can I know it's the best if I don't know what's out there? How can I expect to give great insights if I don't surround myself with great insights first? Just like the skyscraper approach, we need to know what "best" looks like if we want to take its place.

If I take three hours to write a blog post, I ensure that I've recently consumed a minimum of six hours of content on the topic.

Recency is key, since most of what we learn is forgotten by the time we need to recall it. If I were to write a blog post on the economic impact of a hike in the minimum wage in Columbus, Ohio, I'd spend the 2:1 ratio at a minimum even though I wrote about the topic in a research paper in college seven years prior. If I had zero experience, I'd spend much more time on this and also be sure to cite sources at a much higher rate than I would on a topic that I had a large amount of personal experience with.

This rule doesn't apply to content that is made for entertainment or to simply document something that doesn't require "right and wrong" explanations.

Chapter Summary

- Competition is inevitable, but we can leverage it to our advantage with the skyscraper approach.
- The skyscraper approach refers to creating content that is better than the existing top pieces on that topic.
- The skyscraper approach can be applied to any of the three mediums (audio, video, or writing), but it is particularly valuable in writing and search engine optimization.
- Consume more than you create. Implement the 2:1 consume to create ratio whenever you create information-driven content.

Curation = Creation and the Paradox of Originality

"Good artists copy, great artists steal."
> —Steve Jobs . . . who stole it from Pablo Picasso . . .
> who stole it from someone else . . .

No one likes a copycat. If you're a true creator, the last thing you want is to be accused of ripping off the work of others. You're a thinker; you don't want to be labeled as intellectually lazy. You want to become respected and trusted, not just for your own ego, but also because you know that trust and respect are at the heart of successful affiliate marketing.

Pay close attention to what I'm about to share because this fear of being a copycat can absolutely destroy your chances of ever creating great content that matters, and it plays a role in your success and gratification as a marketer.

All great content is inspired by other great content. Author Jonathan Lethem put it well when he said that what we call original is "nine out of ten times they just don't know the reference or the original sources involved."[7]

The simplest analogy is genetics. You are the combination of genes from your mother and your father. You're a "remix" of

---

7 Jonathan Lethem, quoted by Austin Kleon, *Steal Like an Artist* (New York: Workman Publishing, 2012), 7.

their traits. They're a "remix" of your grandparents. We're all genetic remixes, and this is exactly how content works.

But how do we do we copy without being copycats? How can we make our content like this genetic analogy?

First, we need to define what copying really is and when it is wrong. If I were to copy the text from a popular blog post and share it on my site as my own, that is copying. That is intellectually lazy, small, and unethical. If you ever copy directly, you need to cite it and credit the creator.

However, if I take an idea shared by someone else and share my take on it, I've started to create something original. This is originality to the lowest degree. I call this "me too" content. It rides someone else's idea and only brings a small bit more to the table. "Hey, look at me too! I also talked about this!" Not as bad as copying, but not original enough for my liking. I haven't brought enough value. If I want this in front of my readers, I should just share the original piece. So what's next? How do I make this truly my own?

I make it my own by adding new blocks. Just like genetics, the more I add, the more different it becomes.

So in this example I would start by implementing my personal writing style. A style that was inspired by the writings of my favorite bloggers and authors such as Nevelle Medhora, Dale Carnegie, James Clear, and many others. Others I can't remember by name, face, or place. People who influenced me in ways I can't even remember or truly put a finger on.

I'd share it with my personality. A personality that was blended from the elements of parents, friends, role models, TV characters, and countless others over my decades of life on this planet.

Next, I'd include my own stories. Stories from my life that are impossible to emulate and by default will be unique. If I don't have them, I might share stories from the experiences of others that are relevant, giving credit along the way of course.

Then I might add my own graphics to the piece. Graphics perhaps in the minimalistic style from one of my favorite bloggers, Neville Medhora.

This could go on and on. The steps above aren't the rule; they are an example of the process. Take this process and apply it to your own content. There are literally infinite numbers of ways to remix things to make them original. Remember this: the more things you emulate in creating something, the more unique it becomes.

Oh, and if you're wondering who I "copied" this concept from, it was one of my favorite authors, Austin Kleon, in his book Steal Like an Artist. And I bet he'd be proud I'm implementing what he shared in my own voice.

Using content for inspiration is one thing, but let's talk about the power of simply sharing (curating) the great content you find. This is another topic that causes a lot of creators to withhold a surplus of value that they could be sharing with their followers.

I follow very few people on social media. There is, however, a guy who I don't know in real life and who isn't an influencer but I follow him religiously. He probably has no idea I follow him this intently either. The reason I follow him is that he clearly has a great sense of humor. However, he doesn't make original jokes or write anything himself that is particularly funny. Instead, he's what I call a "meme lord." He clearly spends a lot of time sifting through meme pages and then shares the ones that he finds to be the funniest. Although he doesn't share these memes to get paid, this approach to hunting, gathering, and sharing great content works beautifully in affiliate marketing.

There's a massive misconception that to be a creator you have to create original work and that everything you share needs to come directly from you. It's assumed that your ideas should be original and free from outside influence. This couldn't be further from the truth. Some of the greatest content creators are little more than experts at curating content and ideas from others.

Ask yourself these two simple questions: First, "Why do we create content for our audience?" The answer is to create goodwill that eventually may lead to a business transaction.

Question number two, "Is the only way to create goodwill with your audience to share just the content that you've created?" The answer is absolutely not.

There are no rules about how we create goodwill. Sharing amazing content and introducing our followers to other great content creators is just as valuable as sharing your own content.

I've seen affiliate marketers who make their entire careers as curators of great content. They are like radio DJs who find out the music that the listeners want and they provide it to them. You don't think less of Ryan Seacrest because he doesn't have any of his own songs, do you?

The beautiful thing about content curation is that the quality of the content you share will reflect on you. If someone created the world's most thought-provoking and interesting piece of content that your readers adore, they will remember you if you're the one who shared it with them.

Some insecure content creators fear that by sending people to other influencers in their space, they risk losing business. This has never been my experience. Adopt an abundance mentality with sharing great content and don't withhold share-worthy things from your audience just because you're afraid you'll lose their attention going forward to other creators.

Chapter Summary

- Everything is a remix. Stop worrying about being original for originality's sake. Don't blindly copy, but do leverage the inspirations around you to create your own unique voice.

- Sharing great content from other creators can be just as valuable as sharing your own content.
- Focus on providing value rather than hiding great content created by your competitors. There is plenty of traffic to go around, and providing amazing content to your followers will pay off in the long run, even if you lose a little attention by introducing your followers to your content competitors.

Water the Old Content to Maximize Organic Traffic

This chapter refers only to content that is indexed in search engines such as Google or YouTube. Updating old content is unnecessary for social media. In many cases, updating social media content can actually have a negative impact on visibility.

SEO-focused marketers roll their eyes when they hear people say things like "blog posts are free, passive traffic." We know that there is no such thing as free traffic. Maintaining high rankings in search engines requires ongoing work. This is great for the content consumer, but it does make things a bit more difficult on those of us looking to get organic traffic.

We've already discussed the skyscraper approach and how to use it to outrank other websites on search engines. Unfortunately, you and I aren't the only ones aware of this strategy. If you're getting high-quality traffic from competitive search terms, you have a target on your chest. Other SEOs are slicing and dicing your content, trying to find ways to bump themselves over you. If you don't continually update and optimize old content, you'll lose in the long run. Content creators are in a balancing act of creating new content AND updating existing content. Anyone who focuses solely on creating new content is missing out on traffic and conversions.

You can technically optimize all of your content using only

free analytics tools (at the time of this writing that is Google Analytics and Google Search Console), but there are just too many great paid tools out there to ignore.

Once you have your data, it's time to filter it and use it to make decisions. We simply can't always update every single piece of content (at least not in a timely manner), so we need to prioritize what gets the most attention. Curse our finite human condition and the limitations of time!

You'll want to update content that meets the following criteria: it must target your audience, deserve to be its own piece of content, and have a true chance of getting traffic.

1. Targets Your Audience

Many times I've created content that drove organic traffic but later I found out it wasn't traffic that fit my site. This happens if you misinterpret the search intent of a search term you're targeting. Ironically, I've come to despise several pieces of content that started ranking for terms that didn't apply to my topics. Those pieces I don't prioritize updating.

2. Deserves to Be Its Own Article

Some content is better removed or consolidated with other content. In many cases, combining articles into one longer, more complete article is far better than optimizing two separate articles that may be competing with one another.

3. Stands a Reasonable Chance of Getting Traffic

In a perfect world we'd optimize blog posts consistently over long periods of time in hopes of eventually ranking for high volume, highly competitive, highly valuable terms. In reality, some terms are just so far out of reach that it's an inefficient use of your time. If your website is relatively new and the page has very few backlinks, it's unlikely you'll compete for a term like "best flight deals" anytime soon (if ever). Using any research tool, you'll be able to see that the pages ranking for such terms have so many backlinks and are so powerful that it would take an SEO army to take their spot.

For this reason, I like to focus on articles that are ranking just outside the top six spots in search engines. Articles ranking between seven to twenty spots is the range I'm looking for. If I can get these articles moved into the top six, I can easily see huge gains in traffic far more quickly. Roughly two-thirds of all clicks will go to the top six, so I want to be in that group as quickly as possible. This is low-hanging fruit and will give me the most bang for my buck (or time).

From there, we can break these down into three types of content.

1. **Content with high traffic but low conversion rates.** We should focus on improving the conversions here to capitalize on the high traffic.
2. **Content with low traffic but high conversion rates.** We should focus on improving traffic to capitalize on the high conversion rates.
3. **Content that was popular but has declined.** We need to find out why this content has tanked. The best approach will be to use the skyscraper approach in reverse. (This was described earlier in "Skyscraper Approach.")

Content optimizing comes in two forms: defending your rankings and fighting for improved rankings.

If your article is number one in search engines for a key term, you're on defense. If your article isn't as high as you'd like, you're on offense. Both strategies are similar in that you're working to improve your content for search engines, but how you do it is slightly different.

For articles you're defending, you want to see which competitors are gaining on you and why. What have they done that appears to be driving them up the page? Isolate it and see if your page is doing that as well. If not, consider updating your content to do it.

This might include:

- updating your META data (title and description)
- making content longer
- answering specific questions
- formatting in a better way

The adjustments you should make aren't a perfect science. A change you see as an improvement might actually harm your rankings. My suggestion is this: focus on user intent and ask yourself, "Is my article better than all the others at answering the question being asked in the search term?" All search terms are questions after all, even if they don't have question marks. Someone typing in "dog bones" is likely looking for answers to questions about the best dog bones on the market, even though they didn't word it that way.

For articles that you're looking to raise up the search engine rankings, you want to utilize the skyscraper approach outlined in the earlier chapter.

For all posts (defending or raising) you should be doing the following:

- building backlinks
- ensuring content is up to date
- ensuring your calls to action are optimized and click through rates and conversion rates are improved

- ensuring page is user friendly
- ensuring information is still accurate and applicable

Forgetting to optimize old content is like doing a ninety-day work-out program and expecting to keep your newfound abs for life with no additional work.

Chapter Summary

- Regularly updating old content is an often overlooked aspect of driving organic traffic.
- Keep, kill, or consolidate your best pieces regularly.
- If you aren't updating your content, know that someone else is, and they will eventually work to take your positions in search engines.
- Be sure to download the content updating checklist at https://evergreenaffiliatemarketing.com/downloads.

Low-Hanging Fruit on Search Engines

If you are selling something with a piece of content (blog post or video), there are certain keywords that you want your piece to show up for in order to make sales. I call these "buyer intent keywords."

There are three different keywords that people look for in search engines (Google and YouTube are the two powerhouses we focus on primarily as affiliates) that signal what we call "high buyer intent."

1. **Solution Seeking Terms.** The searcher doesn't yet know what products solve their problem. If they are searching from a phrase like "how to get more email opt-ins," we would attract these people with a post like "Using Thrive Leads to Get More Opt-Ins."

2. **Shopping Around Keywords.** The searcher knows the solution they need but wants to learn more about the specific products that can solve it. They also will want to compare solutions that promise the same thing to decide which is best for them.

3. **"At the Register" Keywords.** The searcher has decided they want the product and are looking for a discount or special offer.

The best way to find your buyer intent keywords is to start with your product in mind. Let's say that your product is a program that teaches people how to become better singers called the "Superior Singing Method" (it's a real program at the time of this writing but I know nothing about it). Solution comparison keywords we'd like to rank for could include:

- "How to improve singing voice"
- "Increase vocal range"
- "How to sing better fast"
- "Sing better"

These are very basic phrases and aren't extremely "hot," but if you show up for these sorts of search terms organically, you will be able to pitch your affiliate solution (no pun intended) to people who possibly are in the market for your product.

To create a long list of these solution comparison keyword phrases, start with your product and think of all the different benefits it has and then identify the corresponding search terms that could showcase it.

Next, we have shopping around and comparison research. These keywords are searched by people who know what the solution looks like but they have multiple choices and want to narrow them down.

Keyword phrases for this type include.

- [Affiliate keyword] + "Review"
- [Affiliate keyword] + "Pricing"
- [Affiliate keyword] + "Features" [Competitor] + "Alternative"
- "Product X vs. Product Y"

Finally, we have "at the checkout" keywords. There are four core keywords that when paired with your affiliate product title get traffic that is ready to buy. You should try to incorporate these into your content and consider running traffic to the long tail keywords you make with them.

- [Affiliate keyword] + "Offer"
- [Affiliate keyword] + "Coupon"
- [Affiliate keyword] + "Discount"
- [Affiliate keyword] + "Promo"

These words are powerful because they target only buyers who are extremely close to buying. Getting exposure to these types of search terms will dramatically increase conversions, even without changing anything else about how you're selling your affiliate offers.

This might get me kicked out of some of my favorite copywriting groups, but I need to tell you something very important that is often misunderstood. We're going to cover copywriting in great detail later in this book, but it's not actually the most important thing you do as affiliate marketers. Getting someone to go from a "no" to a "yes" when it comes to buying your affiliate products is great, but it's not the primary means of making sales. Many marketers over-romanticize the power of copywriting and miss a massive shortcut that makes copywriting far less important.

Copywriting isn't king; targeting is king. Finding the people who are already saying "yes" and getting your affiliate links in front of them before your competitors can is the ultimate affiliate growth hack. These low-hanging fruit keywords are a perfect example of finding customers who are already sold and getting in front of them before your competitors. This is far easier than convincing people that they need or want it. Find the people who are "no-brainers" for your product.

Chapter Summary

- Not all search terms are created equal. Some are much more likely to lead to sales.
- The three types of high-buyer-intent keywords are solution seeking, shopping around, and at the checkout.
- Rank in search engines for as many of these low-hanging fruit, high-buyer-intent terms as possible.

Low-Hanging Fruit on Social Media

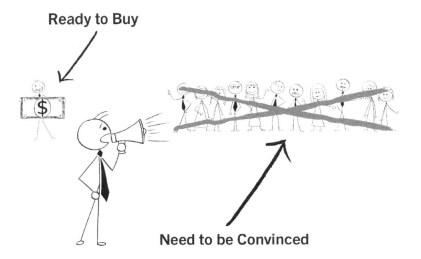

We've discussed the low-hanging fruit keyword terms, but finding easy high-buyer-intent audiences goes much further. We can find the groups of people who are most likely to purchase from us if we put more effort into our research.

Here's a real-world example of great targeting being far more important than sales copy. A successful affiliate marketing friend of mine had a large following in the self-publishing niche. He was promoting a course that teaches writers how to use a complex writing software called Scrivener. Although he did work to sell the course to his own audience, his conversions were starting to dwindle and he wanted to proactively scale further. To do this, he created simple ads to his course review article and targeted them toward anyone who liked the official Scrivener page as well as anyone inside of Scrivener-related pages. Although the page had a relatively small reach, only users of the software would be interested in this product. If it wasn't going to sell to people in this group, it wasn't going to sell anywhere.

Great sales copy wouldn't have a chance at saving this ad campaign. You'd have to convince anyone who sees your ad of several things. They would need to be convinced that they want to write a book, that Scrivener is the best solution for helping them do that, and finally that they should purchase the course you're promoting to learn how to use it.

This isn't to suggest that copywriting doesn't matter. It does. However, great copywriting won't fix bad targeting, but great targeting can hide bad copywriting.

When I bought my first nice car, I already knew which one I wanted. I even had the VIN handy. When I arrived at the dealer, the salesman made one of the easiest sales of his life. I was already sold, he just happened to be in the position to capitalize on it.

How does this apply to affiliate marketing? Just as the car salesman put himself in a position to capitalize on the fact I was already sold, we can put our links in front of people who are ready to buy. Finding them is just as important if not more important than convincing them to buy.

Often times, affiliate marketers spend tremendous amounts of effort working on sales copy but they're attracting the wrong type of traffic. Great copywriting can't solve bad targeting. Before you work on creating amazing copy, make sure that it's getting in front of the right people. Skip ahead and work to find these groups of hot buyers first and the impact of your copywriting will be negligible.

Chapter Summary

- Getting in front of people who are already prepared to buy your affiliate product should be the top priority, and copywriting comes after that.
- Social media platforms give us the information we need to find high-buyer-intent visitors. We just need to put it together.
- Work just as hard to find the "hot" traffic buyers as you do on creating sales copy to push them to buy.

Going Beyond Review Posts

The review post is one of the most common and straightforward tactics used by affiliate marketers to sell their affiliate products. Many affiliate marketers (present company included) have done very well with these types of pieces (blog and video content included).

However, things are changing. The basic review post isn't as effective as it once was, so this chapter will show you what to do instead. The review post is dying for a two reasons.

First, they've been abused and aren't as trustworthy as they once were. Most reviews are written by people wearing rose-tinted glasses (metaphorical of course). Their reviews are little more than biased ads from affiliates like me. The public understands this; they aren't dumb.

Affiliate marketing as a system is to blame for this, but it is the nature of the beast.

This doesn't mean that all reviews are fake or that everyone doing them is shady. It just means that the public is less swayed by a post at the top of Google promising an honest review than it once was. There is just too much incentive for people to hyperbolize for a buck. Ranking on page 1 for an affiliate product review search term usually means some commissions. It's hard to take up that valuable real estate just to give a poor review of the product and not sell anything.

For instance, I rank on page 1 on Google for many high-value terms for a solo service called Udimi. I wish very much that Udimi worked well so I could use them and refer them. They have a great affiliate program and I could have made bank. But alas, the service is bad and the concept of solo ads is flawed.

If I didn't care about my reputation and the value of my brand, I could have easily spun the article to end up promoting Udimi. This is like the other abused post type—the "Don't Buy (Lucrative Affiliate Product) Until You Watch This" content. It's cheesy and overplayed.

The second reason that review posts aren't as effective is because they are boring. We're spoiled by click worthy headlines. We just like things to get our attention and make our decisions on what to click on easier.

Most of the affiliate products that I buy aren't a result of review posts anymore. They're from something like a review post, but more entertaining. That brings me to the review post alternative that will work better. Instead of a straightforward review post, share your product experience differently. It doesn't have to be a formal review to have the same effect that review posts once did. Here's a recent example that got me to buy a product called the Whoop band.

This made me buy

https://medium.com › the-reason-i-bought-a-whoop-is-...   ⋮
The reason I bought a WHOOP is not the reason I'm keeping it ...
WHOOP is not your typical wristband. It's a performance management system that includes hardware (the strap), software (a mobile and a web app), and a ...

https://breakingeighty.com › whoop-review   ⋮
Whoop Review: Is it the Fitness Tracker of Your Dreams? -
Oct 27, 2020 — In this **Whoop** Review I look at whether this new fitness tracker is a huge upgrade or a waste of your time. ... They've **got** major celebrities like Justin Thomas singing it's praises, ... With that said, let's jump into **the why** of all that.
★★★★⯊ Rating: 8.8/10   1 review

I didn't even click this

The article was written on Medium by someone I had never heard of. Since the article told about his unique experience though, I didn't feel like I needed to know him to trust him. The post didn't read like a salesy review; it read like a story—a real human experience.

At the time, it ranked on page 1 of Google for "Whoop," just below the brand itself. It was getting about 2,100 organic visits per month and many more via social. Oh, and the article doesn't even include affiliate links. It could have and would have made a lot of sales.

This type of post solved the two big issues regular reviews have. I didn't feel the need to trust him since it wasn't a straight review post. It wasn't boring at all. The headline had intrigue and made me want to click.

Here's another example of an article ranking on page 1 for a massively profitable search term P90X.

I Failed P90x and Here's What You Can Learn From My ...
https://wanderingaimfully.com › p90x ▾
P90x isn't for everyone. I only made it to P33x, but I did learn a bunch of lessons along the way about life, business, and the **P90x** schedule.

Although this post didn't have an affiliate link selling P90X, it could have and many people would have bought it. Yes, even though the article is about why it didn't work, it could have easily been written to show who P90X would work for based on the writer's personal failure. Beachbody affiliates would KILL for that page 1 real estate.

Here are some headline alternatives you can try instead of the basic "Product + Review + Year + Buzzwords." These have the same selling power as review posts but are less salesy and much more interesting.

Example 1. *I didn't expect this to happen when I started using (product).*

This headline elicited curiosity. Be wary of this sort of headline, though, if you can't deliver on it. If people quickly see it was a bait-and-switch to promote an affiliate, they will bounce right back into the search and your rankings will suffer.

Example 2. *Why is no one talking about this (product) feature?*

For more expensive products, it's highly likely that people have already read multiple reviews. An article like this one will draw attention to something that the others aren't covering. This makes me want to click.

Example 3. *Doing this one thing paid off my (product) subscription for (time).*

If your product is in the B2B space, showing how you used it to quickly recoup the costs is wildly effective.

Example 4. *(#) ways to use (product) for (results).*

This sort of headline helps the prospective buyer visualize themselves using the product and seeing the results.

Example 5. *I almost gave up on (product) and then this happened.*

This sort of headline shows the author had legitimate doubts but overcame them. This is a powerful tactic in persuasion since it makes you far more relatable to the reader. It shows that you aren't shying away from the drawbacks and that you had reservations as well but you found a solution.

Example 6. *(#) reasons why I finally switched to (product).*

This works in the same way as the previous headline because it shows we were hesitant at first but had to cave given the overwhelming supporting information. Simply saying, "It was exactly as amazing as I expected and I had no doubts at all," isn't as compelling to someone who does have doubts. This sounds unreliable to them, so they are less likely to give much weight to your opinion.

These headlines all include the product name for SEO purposes. You will still want to rank for the product name and will want that in the headline. For emails and social, you can completely remove the name to add to the intrigue.

For inspiration, pay attention to a lot of the social ads you see across Facebook, Pinterest, and Instagram. This one for example, "6 Reasons People Are Switching to This Clean Deodorant." If you added the brand name, "[Bravo Sierra] 6 Reasons People Are Switching to This Clean Deodorant," you've got yourself a nice blog headline.

If you're doing any sort of review post or review alternative post, doing the following things will help you make more sales.

1. Stop Reviewing Only the Things That Pay You

As I've said before, our followers aren't dumb. Just because an article doesn't directly sell something doesn't mean it's a waste of time. Some reviews are just great for driving traffic and building goodwill with your readers. And you can leverage the fact that you aren't an affiliate in the title.

2. Stop Giving Everything Rave Reviews

Personally, I have a hard time bashing people's products or services. Luckily, there are enough out there that really earn the bad reviews they get.

Making a bad review is an opportunity for promoting a better alternative inside the post. This could be an affiliate product. Be careful though, because you can look like a real jerk if you're unfairly burning your competitors to sell your own affiliate products. If you're going to do reviews, you need to accept that some things won't be great and you have to be honest about that.

3. Do Your Research and Share Examples

Kill the doubt people may have that your review is fake by sharing real-world examples of how you're using the product or service you're promoting. Show your results. It's hard to argue with results. We will cover this in more detail in the next chapter.

Chapter Summary

- Review posts will always work, but they are no longer the best way to make affiliate sales.
- Separate yourself from competitors on search engines by creating titles that draw intrigue.
- Review things that don't pay you and be honest about the quality. Don't be afraid to give a poor review.
- Deep dive research and examples makes review posts far more compelling.

Go Really Deep

Every product you promote likely has dozens if not hundreds of other hungry affiliates who are creating unoriginal, "me too" content to drive sales. This is good for you because you can separate yourself from the herd quickly by going deeper than your competitors. Anything you promote has an opportunity for deeper content. Here's what I mean.

Let's say that you promote a dietary supplement that helps people enter ketosis quickly. Instead of just making a blog or video gushing about how great the product is, prove it. Compare it to the alternatives and show the results.

Titles for this sort of piece of content could be something like, "I Tried Ten Different Ketone Drinks; Here's Which Ones Actually Work." This will also make you far more confident when selling the product. You have concrete proof that your product is actually superior, and you saw it with your own eyes.

This testing and researching method applies to far more than just health products. I switched my website's hosting provider after reading an extremely well-done deep dive test a blogger created testing all the big name hosting providers on the market. He created test sites, purchased every major hosting plan, and showed the unedited results in a very compelling, easy-to-consume way.

He showed me with real data why the product he was promoting was actually superior. This is the apex of affiliate marketing: doing deep research that the average person wouldn't have time to do in order to prove which products are superior. There's a reason companies like Consumer Reports thrive on this sort of testing and sharing model—it flat out works.

After reading the hosting review, I was relieved to buy it and the decision was a no brainer. The craziest part was that I wasn't even totally unsatisfied with my original hosting service. I wasn't in the market to switch until the article hit me with rock solid data showing that I was leaving money on the table by not switching.

Chapter Summary

- One of the greatest values you can give as an affiliate marketer is to do deep testing of the products you promote and sharing the results.
- Showing quantifiable proof that your affiliate product is superior will make it easy to drive sales, even to people who didn't know they even needed the product.

TACTICS AND STRATEGY

Have Your Own Product

Part of the allure of affiliate marketing is that you don't have to be the one to deliver on the purchase or provide additional customer support. You can make the sale and refer all questions to the company (although I explain later on why you should take a more active approach to this sort of thing). The premise is beautiful, so what I'm about to say may be a little unappealing. But I promise; it has tremendous benefits.

Creating your own product gives you a huge advantage over affiliates who don't have one. Here's why.

1. Customers of Your Products Turn into the Highest Quality of Owned Traffic

When I've run affiliate programs for businesses, I always attempt to get other businesses that serve the same market to promote for them. These are often the "big fish" when it comes to affiliate promoters because they have access to the best traffic possible. Their traffic is made up of the people who are in the niche and have shown they're serious enough to spend money.

You'd be shocked at how many companies that seem small on the surface can drive massive sales if they promote an affiliate offer. As you might expect, the more expensive the product they sell, the more sales they can drive because they've attracted the absolute cream of the crop in terms of people who are serious and willing and able to spend money.

You've likely heard the saying, "Your best future customers are your current customers," or, "It's exponentially less expensive to keep a customer than acquire a new one." If you have a product, you create customers and customers create future sales. Having a large buyer list is usually far more valuable than having a large list that was built by giving away freebies or hosting webinars.

2. A Product Can Grow Your Reputation and Site Authority

A common theme of this book is that great affiliate marketers build and leverage trust. Something strange happens when someone has trusted you with even a small amount of money (even just one dollar). They have now made a physical acknowledgment that they trust you at least a bit. Cognitive bias will make them like and trust you more since part of their own ego is now tied to you. If it sounds like I'm over-thinking this, you'll understand better when you see this for yourself. Conversion rates are often three times higher for my past buyers of any products than they are for people who have never purchased.

3. Products Can Be Used as Bonuses to Promote Affiliate Products

You'll learn more about bonuses in a later chapter, but having your own product gives you something to give away. If you have a quality product that is worth $99 (actually worth $99 and is selling for that price regularly) you can give it away to people who purchase an affiliate product that pays you out $299 (rough example).

Assuming that the products you're giving away have a low cost to you and high margins, you can see a massive increase of conversions for a slightly reduced ROI. We'll go over how to do this effectively in a later chapter, "Boost Conversions with Bonus Stacks."

4. Affiliate Offers Can Be Added As "Thank You Page Upsells"

If the idea of creating a single product is daunting, the idea of creating a full-scale sales funnel with upsells, downfalls, and bump offers might seem downright impossible. Although having a fine-tuned sales funnel is one of the best things you can do to maximize your product's earning potential, you don't need one to make more revenue from each sale you drive thanks to affiliate offers.

One of my favorite things to do is to add an affiliate recommendation that compliments my product perfectly on my thank you page. It's essentially free real estate for promotion, and it catches your buyers when they are in a buyer state. The hardest part is pulling out the credit card, but once it's out, people are more likely to buy related offers. This includes affiliate offers.

The flow looks something like this:

Your Landing Page → Your Sales Page → Thank You Page with Low-Pressure Affiliate Offer

Yes, this is imperfect for several reasons, and your conversion rates will be lower on the affiliate offer than if you actually sold the product on your funnel since they have to actively choose to buy or decline. However, the conversion rates on these thank you page offers are higher than when I post them elsewhere. Leveraging the attention of a buyer who is in a buying mood is going to drive your affiliate sales. It might even drive more profits for you than the actual product itself!

Making a product in the twenty-first century is far easier than many people think. I've created dozens of products of all different types over the years. If needed, I could have a product up and running in just a few hours, although you do not need to rush this process.

The best products are things that can be delivered virtually that don't cost you much in terms of ongoing support or actual costs. They also should be relevant to the target audience of your affiliate promotions. For example, I wouldn't want to create a web course on mastering Excel if my niche is fitness and health. Using the health and fitness industry as an example, I'd want my product to be something like "Printable 30-Day Arm Workouts" or maybe a web course on how body builders can use yoga to increase their gains, reduce injury, and minimize soreness.

Here are just some examples:

- web course
- software
- e-book
- coaching (not the best, since it requires a fixed amount of time)
- printable resources
- membership access

The list is endless. If you need motivation, consider the things you promote and think what else someone who would buy those might also want.

Chapter Summary

- Although one beauty of affiliate marketing is that you don't have the same hassles that product owners have to deal with, having your own product can be a tremendous asset.
- People who buy your products are far more likely to buy your affiliate offers as well in the future.
- You can use your own products as bonus offers when customers purchase your other affiliate products.

Pixel Everything

Let this stat sink in: Between "70 to 96% of the visitors abandoning your site will never return."[8] With the nonstop battle for attention, this is only going to get higher over time.

This isn't because your content isn't good either. It's just how things are. As of 2021, there are over 600 million blogs[9] and 1.8 billion websites.[10] Video is even more competitive, with over 500 hours' worth of content being uploaded to YouTube every minute.[11]

People would likely love to see your content or offer again, but most of them won't remember your URL on their own. Unless you're a name brand website or a celebrity (with an easy-to-spell name), you need to get your content in front of the visitor again.

We can do this with tracking pixels. Tracking pixels install "cookies" on the browser of the person who visited your page. Anyone who has been cookied can be re-marketed to.

8 Jonathan Long, "Is Your Website Acting as Customer-Repellent? Avoid These 5 Don'ts," Entrepreneaur, August 18, 2014, https://www.entrepreneur.com/article/236548.

9 Kyle Byers, "How Many Blogs Are There? (And 141 Other Blogging Stats)," GrowthBadger, January 23, 2021, https://growthbadger.com/blog-stats.

10 "Total Number of Websites," Internet Live Stats, accessed June 29, 2021, https://www.internetlivestats.com/total-number-of-websites.

11 James Hale, "More than 500 Hours of Content Are Now Being Uploaded to YouTube Every Minute," Tubfilter, May 7, 2019, https://www.tubefilter.com/2019/05/07/number-hours-video-uploaded-to-youtube-per-minute/#:~:text=The%20platform's%20users%20upload%20more,of%20new%20content%20per%20day.

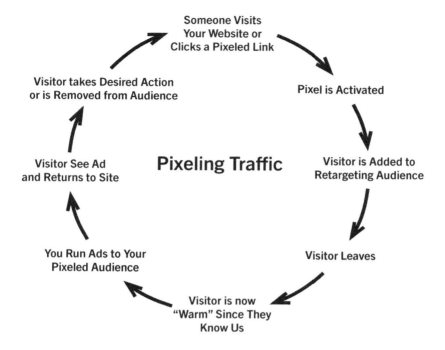

Think of things like this:

- Using a social media ad to promote an affiliate with exclusive bonuses to anyone who viewed a related blog post.
- Promote a lead magnet to visitors who read an article but don't subscribe.
- Boost other non-sales focused content to get them to return and build your relationship together.

The possibilities are endless, but unfortunately, tracking has become increasingly harder each year. Depending on when you're reading this, tracking might be far more limited than it was when this was written. If there is any form of tracking left (there will be something), use it. Data and information are so valuable, they're nearly currency on their own.

Chapter Summary

- Most of your website visitors will never come back. Pixeling traffic allows us to get a second exposure to our visitors.
- Pixeled traffic is very valuable because it is warm. Visitors are somewhat familiar with you since they've visited your website or engaged with you wherever your pixel has been placed.

Fight for a Coupon Code

Few things will help you make more affiliate sales than a unique coupon code for the products you promote. The logic is relatively simple. Make a better offer and see better conversions. A coupon code does more than that, though, for affiliate marketers. Coupon codes help us drive more conversions without requiring clicks to our affiliate links.

If sales that use the coupon code are automatically assigned to you (which is typically the case), you'll keep a larger portion of the sales you send since the coupon should override any other tracking IDs. You can make sales even if the buyer doesn't use your link as long as they use your code. This is important for affiliate marketers who leverage audio or video platforms where clicking links is not as common.

It's worth asking the affiliate manager if this is the case or not. A great program should do this, but they don't always. Don't feel bad working hard for a discount either. Offering deals is far from a one-sided exchange of value. There are tons of companies out there dying to give you and your audience amazing deals just for the exposure. I know this because I do it with my own products!

Let's say that you have a Facebook group for bodybuilders and I'm the owner of a new subscription service that provides ready-to-eat, high-protein meals to your door. The lifetime value of a customer is extremely high for me; the struggle is getting people to try out the service.

151

Striking a deal together would be an absolute win-win. My readers would get more value (discount); I get more sales thanks to the discount and so does the company giving the discount.

Most affiliate programs will allow you to tell them what you'd like your coupon code to be. If given the option, make sure that the code is short, easy to spell, and memorable.

For example, a coupon for 10% of for my readers titled NM10 is short, easy to remember and easy to spell. My initials plus the percentage off all in a short code that is easy to type manually. If my coupon code was something like RJ329F2 or 112-483Z, I'd make far fewer sales. Again, this is particularly valuable if you are a podcaster or video marketer who needs to relay your code quickly and easily so your followers can type it in.

Chapter Summary

- Coupon codes make it far easier to drive conversions to any affiliate product.
- Coupon codes can help increase conversions by ensuring they credit you with sales even if your affiliate link wasn't clicked.
- Make sure that, if possible, you have a unique coupon code created for your audience.
- If possible, make sure that your coupon code is short, easy to spell, and memorable.

Boost Conversions with Bonus Stacks

"For it is in giving that we receive."

—Francis of Assisi

This is one of my all-time favorite pieces of affiliate marketing advice. I highly recommend that you implement the methods I'm going to teach you as soon as possible. They are applicable to anyone selling just about anything. And as marketers we can give our audience more while simultaneously growing our businesses.

Most affiliate offers are highly competitive. Even if you have a large audience, established credibility, and goodwill with your followers, some affiliate products are destined to underperform due to extreme competition. That is, of course, assuming you do nothing to give yourself a competitive advantage. The advantage is this: bring something more to the offer than just the affiliate product.

We bring more to the offer by adding our own unique bonuses that we deliver to anyone who purchases products through our affiliate links. By doing this, we can easily get followers who are on the fence of purchasing to fully commit and buy.

Most people are on the verge of buying but never do. Most affiliates ignore these people. You and I will use them as our core audience.

Bonuses can ethically instill FOMO (Fear of Missing Out) within your audience. FOMO is an important part of marketing.

It is important that we give our buyers a reason to buy now. Don't guilt yourself over this. If you're selling something worth buying, there is nothing wrong with giving users an extra nudge to stop dragging their feet. Your true fans will appreciate this.

Good bonus packages should improve on the product, increasing the chances of success and decreasing the risk of failure when using the item you're promoting.

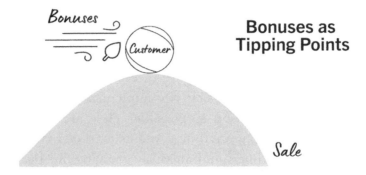

With one affiliate product in mind, ask yourself the following questions:

- What is the ROI on an affiliate sale?
- What ROI would you accept?

With affiliate products, the ROI is generally very high. Unless you are spending a fortune on paid ads, your affiliate ROI is measured relative to the time and energy you put into creating content to push the affiliate organically.

You should use bonuses when your margins are enough that you can afford to give more in exchange for more sales. Don't over-utilize this approach or it will lose its effectiveness.

Now it's important to note that you can't use the bonus method so much that the prices of the things you're giving away as bonus products become permanently damaged. If every single time you promote an affiliate product you offer the same bonuses at the same massive discounts, your loyal followers will start to catch on to this and will think your prices are artificially inflated since you love giving them away so often.

There are a few keys to a good bonus offer:

1. Make it relevant to the product you're selling.
2. Give it a monetary value.
3. Make sure it improves the results of the main product.

The best way to create bonus offers is by throwing in your own products. These can come in the form of digital products like software or courses. If you have your own products, you can also give discounts as bonuses. This will not only boost conversions but will also add extra revenue on top of it.

If you don't have products, that is okay; there are other options.

- one-on-one training
- purchase other products for them
- partner with another product creator

Give enough to offset the potential lost sales from bonuses plus some. As long as you are making more money, adding bonuses means happier customers (they are getting more bang for their buck), and you are coming out on top.

If you are part of a massive affiliate launch and there are a number of other affiliates also offering bonuses, you need to make yours stick out. In cases where commissions are huge ($1,000+), throwing in "everything but the kitchen sink" may be necessary to compete.

If you need to give too much to get a sale and compete, bow out. Don't lose money just for the sake of beating other affiliates.

The Bonus Strategy That Helped Me Win a Mercedes

This strategy helped me win a Mercedes Benz, so pay attention. It's quick, but it may be the most valuable takeaway you get from this entire book.

Membership programs are an amazing way to earn recurring income. In 2017 I created one with a unique twist. Instead of asking people to pay me each month, I asked them to purchase a software through my affiliate link instead.

To join my membership group, they just had to forward me their receipt to prove they purchased. As an added benefit, I was able to show people how to use the software in my group! This meant they were more likely to remain members even after the program ended.

My big mistake was making the program finite. I set a ninety-day end date, and as you can imagine, a lot of people canceled afterward. Still, I earned a nice payday and later refined the method to make it work in other niches.

Chapter Summary

- Adding incentives for anyone who purchases through your affiliate links is an amazing way to boost conversions, increase retention, and make your customers happy.
- A good bonus stack should be relevant to the affiliate product and help achieve the desired results faster, easier, or with less money.

Free Courses That Support Buyers

We mentioned how creating content to help train your referrals on how to get the most out of the product they purchased can help with retention, but we can leverage training to sell affiliate products as well. Typically, you can make more money selling a digital for what it's actually worth, but sometimes creating a short course and adding relevant affiliate links to the content can make you more in the long run. Free courses can also help grow your email list and build tremendous goodwill with your followers.

One of the big hang-ups people have with buying something is they fear: "I don't really think I'll be able to use this," or "I need to see more real-world examples of how this will benefit me." If you truly believe in a product you're promoting, this will shine through in your free coursework.

The sales are much easier, but the difficult part is getting people to actually go through the course content. No matter what you're teaching, the completion rate will often be closer to 0% than it is to 100%. That is unless you make it a priority to get people to really go through your content in its entirety.

This is why shorter courses that teach something very specific are more likely to drive conversions. Focus not only on getting people to enroll but also to actually go through the content. This is to their benefit and yours since they won't even see your affiliate offers unless they progress through the course.

Creating a course doesn't need to be complicated. You can use a basic Wordpress plugin or pay for something that is a bit more sophisticated. You can even create a course that is delivered in the form of an email sequence.

Chapter Summary

- Creating free or low-cost courses to teach people how to use the products you recommend can lead to affiliate sales as well as increased retention.

Create Free Tools

The word "free" has a different meaning to affiliate marketers. We can give things for free but still drive thousands of dollars' worth of sales from them. One way we can do this is by monetizing our free software with sidebar display ads that pay for clicks or impressions or direct links to other relevant affiliates.

This method requires some creativity, so the best way to help you here is by showing you some real-world examples. One site that does this extremely well is LeanDomainSearch.com. The magic of this site is that it provides a tremendous service and drives BlueHost affiliate commissions whenever someone chooses a domain they like.

The flow is brilliant. People come to the site to find domain name inspiration. Visitors simply type in some core terms like "birds" in the example above and they will be shown a ton of variations of available domain names that include that term. There are some simple filters that can be added to filter and sort the results, but it's nothing crazy.

When someone sees a domain name they like, they click on it to verify that it is in fact available. If it is, they are promoted to purchase the domain on BlueHost. At the time of this writing, BlueHost was paying $65 per sale generated.

The program is free and doesn't even require an email opt-in or show any banner ads on the sidebars. That's a fantastic sign that the affiliate sales are coming in strong.

Free Software for Sales

Next, let's examine a tool created by one of the most successful affiliate marketing companies of all time, NerdWallet.com. They created a calculator that allows visitors to see how much they could save by refinancing. The flow looks like this.

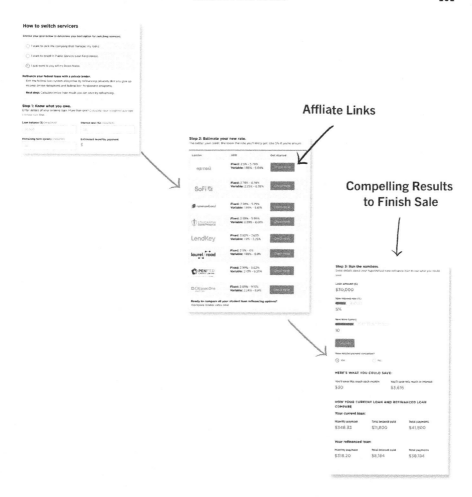

Users share their current loan amounts, interest rates, and remaining loan term. Next, they are shown a list of services that they could use to refinance and have calls to action encouraging them to click to learn more. These are the affiliate links for the tool. Finally, the greatest copywriting of all time: data proving you'll save money. They don't need to do very much more to make a sale here. They can show exactly how much money someone will save by using one of their partner programs.

Let's do one more example. When I'm running Google ad campaigns, I use a free tool called Keywords Toaster to generate different match variations. The only cost to me is that I'm exposed to relevant ads. That is a win in my book all around.

Free Tool

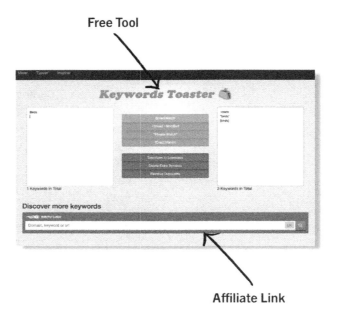

Affiliate Link

Take note of the fact that the affiliate products being promoted in the tools are highly relevant to what the tool does. At the bottom of the window you see SEMRush, which is a tool that, among other things, allows marketers to spy on the Google ad campaigns of their competitors. Someone who uses Keywords Toaster is probably someone who would be in the market to buy SEMRush.

What's especially powerful about these types of programs is that people will likely use them multiple times. More exposure to the affiliate products is always a good thing. If possible, create a tool that is used frequently by the visitor.

Keep in mind, there is a difference between creating a free tool that organically sells an affiliate product and cookie stuffing. Never engage in cookie stuffing. This is the process of creating programs that force your affiliate cookies into user's browsers and credit you for sales that you didn't actually make. This is highly unethical and will almost always result in being permanently banned from the affiliate program if caught.

Chapter Summary

- Free is surprisingly lucrative. Create free tools that attract your potential buyers and organically sell them while they are using the product.
- Tools that are used more than once will increase impressions to your affiliate products and increase conversions. Try to create tools that become part of the user's daily life or workflow.
- Never engage in cookie stuffing. This is unethical and is always against the affiliate program's terms of service.

Make a "Blue Ocean"

Affiliate marketing is a cutthroat business. No matter what you're promoting, competition is inevitable. This is why we need to do everything in our power to create our own markets that are devoid of competition.

W. Chan Kim calls this the "blue ocean strategy" and he explains the process in his book Blue Ocean Shift.

> "Blue ocean shift is a systematic process to move your organization from cutthroat markets with bloody competition—what we think of as red oceans full of sharks—to wide-open blue oceans, or new markets devoid of competition, in a way that brings your people along."[12]

One way to create a blue ocean is to find a new audience for a product—an audience that isn't aware of the value of the product because they weren't the originally intended target market. If you can find a way to make the product of value to the new audience that is not being served by the majority of promoters, you can give yourself a real advantage.

---

12 W. Chan Kim and Renee Mauborgne, *Blue Ocean Shift: Beyond Competing— Proven Steps to Inspire Confidence and Seize New Growth* (New York: Hachette Books, 2017), 7.

Here's a real-world example.

I was promoting a wildly popular sales funnel software years ago. The affiliate program was extremely competitive, and everyone was promoting it to internet entrepreneurs who had a digital product to sell. Making sales organically was extremely difficult. So I created a new audience for the product.

I had a large following in the Amazon FBA (fulfillment by Amazon) selling space, and I saw ways that sellers could use the software to sell physical products and get more product reviews. The method was so successful that I was able to sell over 100 new subscriptions and even got a "dream car" award in the process. To date, I'm one of the only people who has taken this angle and the blue ocean remains blue.

Chapter Summary

- Try to carve out a niche that is free from competition.

Be Affiliate #0

"Do not go where the path may lead. Go instead where there is no path and leave a trail."

—Ralph Waldo Emerson

Selling anything is hard enough as it is, but selling a product AND competing with other affiliates selling the exact same product can be grueling work. There's no shame in running away from the competition from time to time by finding opportunities to be the first affiliate of a product. How do you do this? It's pretty easy.

First, find awesome products that don't have affiliate programs yet. You don't even need to go out of your way to do this. The odds are good that there are already a slew of things you use that haven't implemented affiliate marketing into their promotional strategies yet.

Since you're already involved with affiliate marketing, you know enough about the concept to explain how it works to these business owners. Hit them up with the core sales points. Remind them that there is no risk. Affiliates make a sale or they don't get paid.

Find out whether their competitors are using affiliate programs already. If they are, explain why this could help them catch up. If they aren't, explain how if they run one first they could leave their competitors in the dust. You were sold on affiliate marketing at some point; you should be able to sell them. This will create what we call a "blue ocean."

Chapter Summary

- Give yourself a massive advantage by becoming the first affiliate of something.
- Many companies don't understand the power of having an affiliate program or the logistics of getting it running. Show them why they want one and how to set it up.

Show the Hard Way to Sell the Better Way

This is one of my absolute favorite methods for selling affiliate offers through search engines without creating content that is obviously a sales pitch. Here's how it works.

First, you find a product that solves a common problem better than the traditional solution that is more commonly known. For example, if you have a tool or service that makes Microsoft Excel obsolete, this would be a perfect fit for this method.

Go through your existing affiliate products and ask yourself, "What does this replace or improve upon?" The answer is the product we will target.

Next, you find the terms that people are searching when they want help using the existing solution (the product we're replacing). Since our product is an alternative, getting in front of existing users is golden real estate. We do this with headlines like the following:

- "How to (do task) with (common product)"
- "(Common problem) with (common product)"
- "(Common product) Tips"

My favorite is answering common problems when my solution solves them. This is because the user is already aware of the problem and how frustrating it might be. Showing them a better, easier, or faster way to do it makes for easy sales.

If you aren't sure of the common issues people have with the traditional product, try using it extensively yourself. See what sorts of questions you have organically. Make a note of the things you searched for to find answers.

Next, create content for search engines that answers the search query in detail. You will use this opportunity to interject, "If you want an easier way to do this, check out (your affiliate product)," when relevant.

This is especially helpful when the existing product is confusing or has a high learning curve. People are used to getting their answers from search engines. They're already there, we just need to meet them.

Here's how it would look using the Microsoft Excel example. Let's say that I have an affiliate offer I promote that is a monthly done-for-you Excel service. Essentially, it's a way to outsource your Excel tasks to specialists without doing your own hiring.

I'd try to rank for all of the difficult Excel tutorial terms and I'd plug in, "If you don't want to deal with the hassle of doing this yourself, check out (affiliate service). For just $99/month they will handle all of your basic to intermediate Excel tasks. Click here to check them out." This would be added near the top, and I'd also interject something similar at the bottom. Something like, "So it's a bit of a hassle, but that's how to do it if you want to do it on your own. If you don't want to do it and want to save a bunch of time and hassle, check out (affiliate service)."

The beautiful thing about this approach is that the competition is usually far lower since the phrases you're targeting aren't clearly sales focused. It can be your blue ocean and a secret source of sales that competitors don't even notice.

Chapter Summary

- If your affiliate product is a solution to a more commonly used product, create content that answers questions regarding the more common product and use it as an opportunity to introduce your affiliate product.
- Targeting queries that show someone has a problem makes it easy to make sales if your product provides a better solution.

Do Giveaways

Giveaways are great for many reasons. They're so powerful that it's often in my best interest to purchase several of the products I promote (whether they're physical or virtual) just so I can create contests and giveaways to hand them out for free to a few of my followers. This does several things.

First, it helps you build your list. Your list is your cash cow. Contests are like steroids for growing it.

Next, it builds the desire for your product. Have you ever entered to win something, and the contest made you want it even more than before? This anomaly has happened to me many times. If you can make the contest public so others can see how many other people also want the freebie, that will heighten the intrigue and desire even more.

Finally, it brings awareness to your product. People read sales copy differently based on what you're trying to accomplish. If you're trying to get them to pull out a credit card, it might not be as compelling as if you're giving away a select few of an item for free. There are plenty of free and paid ways to run giveaways.

It should go without saying, but don't ever cheat on any contests. I've seen many times—creators run contests and either never pick a winner, pick someone ahead of time, or pick a made-up winner so they don't have to pay anything to deliver. Giving people prizes will increase their chances of becoming real lifetime fans and followers. It's also just the ethical thing to do.

Chapter Summary

- Doing contests and giveaways can grow your email list, make your affiliate product more desirable, and bring more awareness to it.

Leverage Seasonality

Seasonal marketing isn't just important for businesses like Christmas tree lots in December or those pop-up Halloween shops that take over previously vacant buildings in October. Affiliate marketers can leverage seasonality to organically boost their sales if they can find a great angle.

Most affiliate programs run promotions during major holidays, and this can be your chance to capitalize on increased conversion rates. To do this, you need to stay tuned to which of your affiliate products runs promotions and be sure that you don't miss the boat to push them.

Here are my two rules to effectively leveraging seasonality.

Rule 1. Never Be Tacky and Know That Some Days are Always off Limits

Days of mourning are simply off limits. September 11th in the United States seems like an obvious day to abstain from sales promotions and at the very least avoid any silly sales promotions. But somehow, every year multiple companies create distasteful deals like "BOGOs" with images of the twin towers or American flags made out of pizza toppings.

Never under any circumstances attempt to monetize tragedy. This includes things like keeping a promotion going longer than planned because of a recent tragedy like a mass shooting or the death of a highly loved public figure. Just don't do it.

Rule 2. Give Consumers Plenty of Time before the Day

If you're selling products that can be gifted on Mother's Day or Christmas, for example, you won't make many sales if you promote a product on Christmas Eve that requires a week to ship. It seems obvious, and it is, but if you aren't diligent to plan your promotions ahead of time, you'll usually find you remembered too late to really make the offer work.

Chapter Summary

- Plan in advance promotions for different holidays or affiliate program campaigns.
- Be careful to be respectful and never try to monetize a tragedy or somber event.

Low-Ticket Items to Low-Quality Traffic

I learned this from a good friend and super affiliate named Spencer Mecham. As I mentioned earlier, anyone who has ever purchased something from you will be exponentially more likely to buy from you again, and this applies to low-ticket affiliate offers as well.

You want to quickly separate new traffic, followers, or subscribers into buyers and tire kickers. This doesn't mean shoving big-ticket items down their throats nonstop from day one. Instead, offer something that is extremely affordable but packs a lot of value.

Ideally, I try to sell something that is under $30. This could be an e-book, a simple software, or anything relevant to your audience. People who buy this product will quickly join your bucket of serious buyers. As you prune your lists over time, you'll keep these followers since they've shown they are serious.

Chapter Summary

- Sell low-cost items to traffic early to help identify who is serious and who isn't.

COPYWRITING

Eight Desires and Nine Wants

All of copywriting revolves around the eight basic human desires and nine learned wants. In his book *Cashvertising*, Drew Eric Whitman refers to the basic desires as the "Life Force 8." The basic human needs are biologically programed and are powerful desires found in every healthy human being. They are as follows.

- Desire 1. Survival, enjoyment of life, life extension
- Desire 2. Enjoyment of food and drink
- Desire 3. Freedom from fear, pain, and danger
- Desire 4. Sexual companionship
- Desire 5. Comfortable living conditions
- Desire 6. To be superior, winning, and "keeping up with the Joneses"
- Desire 7. Care and protection of loved ones
- Desire 8. Social approval[13]

Why do these matter? Leveraging the Life Force 8 gives you the power of Mother Nature herself. You're tapping into the very essence of what makes us human.

---

13 Drew Eric Whitman, *Cashvertising: How to Use More than 100 Secrets of Ad-Agency Psychology to Make Big Money Selling Anything to Anyone* (Pompton Plains, NJ: Career Press, 2009), 21.

Also, if your copywriting content doesn't focus on at least one of these desires, you won't sell anything. Even if you weren't aware of it, if you've ever sold anything, you likely targeted one or more of these desires. However, being deliberate to target these desires when creating sales content will take the effectiveness of your copy to a new level.

Unlike the Life Force 8, there are 9 Learned Wants that we develop over time. They are as follows:

- Learned Want 1. To be informed
- Learned Want 2. Curiosity
- Learned Want 3. Cleanliness of body and surroundings
- Learned Want 4. Efficiency
- Learned Want 5. Convenience
- Learned Want 6. Dependability and quality
- Learned Want 7. Expression of beauty and style
- Learned Want 8. Economy and profit
- Learned Want 9. Bargains[14]

These learned wants are powerful and can be a very useful part of great copywriting, but they don't hold a candle to the power of the Life Force 8 since they aren't engrained in our DNA. If we fail to focus on the Life Force 8 and just emphasize the 9 Learned Wants, we will not maximize our conversions. For a better idea of why this is, let's juxtapose a few Life Force 8 elements to one of the 9 Learned Wants.

- Would you leave your child in a hot car (Life Force 7) on a summer day to get your hair done (learned want 7)?

---

14 Whitman, *Cashvertising*, 23.

- Would you eat rotten food (Life Force 2) to save money (Learned Want 9)?
- Would you become celibate for life (Life Force 4) if someone paid you to (Learned Want 7)?

With few exceptions, the life force urges will outweigh the learned wants, which we have no biological urge to satisfy but have learned to want them over time. Always focus on the Life Force 8 first and used the learned wants as secondary sales points to get the maximum results from all of your copywriting.

Chapter Summary

- People have eight basic desires that are biologically engrained in our DNA.
- The best advertising appeals to these eight basic desires.
- There are nine learned wants (secondary wants) that are useful in copywriting but are not replacements for the Life Force 8. They are used to supplement the sales message that is woven into one of the Life Force 8 desires.

Kill the $5 Words

"Don't use a five-dollar word when a fifty-cent word will do."
—Mark Twain

As students, we're taught to use big words. While throwing in fancy, uncommon words may help you get a few cheap points on your SAT, it does very little in the real world. This is perhaps one of the greatest disservices done to young writers.

Force this approach out of your mind. Forget what you've been taught up until this point about the importance of big words. It was all nonsense. Having a robust vocabulary is great, but using your full arsenal of fancy languages can be harmful.

No one has ever complained that something was explained too simply. That is, as long as it conveyed everything that it needed to convey. If you can make your content or sales copy easier to read, you'll increase the chances of your potential buyer reading more of it, which then increases the chances that they will buy. So do whatever it takes to make reading easy for them.

Chapter Summary

- Keep your writing as simple as possible without sacrificing accuracy and completeness. No one will complain that something was explained in a way that was too easy to understand.

The "I"s Don't Have It

Before you send an email, publish a social media post, etc., read through it and ask, "Is this about the reader, or is it about me?" Nine times out of ten, it will be about you.

Don't feel bad, it's human nature. Your favorite topic is . . . you! Your readers' favorite topic is . . . them! You won't believe how many "I" statements I had to remove from this book! ← Left this one. ☺

So let's make our readers the star of our content whenever possible. Utilize second person (you) or first person plural (we, us) when possible. This will increase conversions since it will help the reader picture themselves using your product, solving their problems, seeing results, etc.

Likewise, no matter how honest you are, people who don't know you are wise to be apprehensive of your recommendations. We can all tell when someone is paid to promote something. Their word doesn't hold as much weight with us. But the word of other, non-commissioned users does. So when you're creating sales content, leverage the positive feedback of others as often as possible. When it comes to testimonials, stories, and feedback from actual users, adopt a "more is more" strategy. Collect as many as possible and use them liberally.

Chapter Summary

- Everyone cares more about themselves than anything else. Make everything about them.
- Get feedback from users of the products you promote and leverage that in your marketing.

Don't Withhold Drawbacks

No product is perfect. Pretending that all of your affiliated products are perfect will hurt your credibility. Ironically, honestly showcasing the flaws or shortcomings of something you're promoting can improve conversion rates. It will also dramatically decrease your refunds. In affiliate marketing, a refunded product is worse than no sale because you might have damaged the trust level with your follower. Helping someone buy something is great, but helping someone avoid a buying mistake is also great in the long-term since it will build your relationship.

Just from a copywriting perspective, ironically it's less compelling when we present a product as immaculate. Even the best products on the planet have things that could be perceived as negatives. I buy every single Apple product, but I roll my eyes if someone promotes their products as perfect.

Also, drawbacks can vary based on the person. What is a powerful sales point for one person could be a negative for someone else. Explaining the type of people who are good fits or not good fits for your products is extremely valuable.

Here are some examples of qualifiers you may want to use.

Workout Program: "This product is great if you're the type of person who can stick to a very strict routine."

Clothing: "These fit really well if you have a larger frame but might be baggy and uncomfortable for more petite folks."

Expensive Business Software: "If your business is at scale and your growth has flatlined, this could be a good fit. But it's usually overkill for someone new to the industry."

Coaching: "A great opportunity and supplement to growth, but not a replacement for your own elbow grease and experimentation."

Chapter Summary

- Every product has some shortcoming. Addressing these head-on can actually boost your conversion rates.
- Drawbacks aren't universal. What is a positive feature to one person could be a negative to another. Explain who your product is and isn't for. Don't be afraid to lose buyers who aren't a good fit.

Create a "Swipe File"

"The artist is a collector. Not a hoarder, mind you, there's a difference: Hoarders collect indiscriminately, artists collect selectively. They only collect things that they really love. There's an economic theory out there that if you take the incomes of your five closest friends and average them, the resulting number will be pretty close to your own income. I think the same thing is true of our idea incomes. You're only going to be as good as the stuff you surround yourself with. My mom used to say to me, 'Garbage in, garbage out.' It used to drive me nuts. But now I know what she meant. Your job is to collect good ideas. The more good ideas you collect, the more you can choose from to be influenced by."

—Jim Jarmusch

It doesn't matter whether you're a fantastic copywriter or not, you can benefit by leveraging the work of others as inspiration. Save yourself the struggle of writer's block and start collecting every example of great sales copy that you can find. Store it somewhere you can access it later.

Save things like:

- links to great landing pages
- screenshots of amazing email subject lines
- pictures of paid ads that caught your eye

187

Surround yourself with great copy. Follow people who create great sales copy (whether they're in your niche or not). I'm on many random email lists. I receive broadcasts from great advertisers in many different niches even though I'm not particularly interested in what they're selling. Instead, I'm interested in how they're selling it.

Reading great copy from other marketers (especially ones in completely different niches) can give you the steady stream of daily inspiration and ideas needed to create great broadcasts on a consistent basis. Build up your stash of swipe material and you'll find it much easier to create great sales copy more quickly without the mind-numbing pain of writer's block.

Chapter Summary

- Collect things that inspire you and refer to them regularly.
- Anything worth emulating should be added to your swipe file.

Sell the Results Not the Features

"Consumers buy based on what the product will do for them, not on what ingredients it has."
—Newspaper Association of America

This copywriting rule isn't unique to affiliate marketing, but you need to understand it in order to maximize your conversions. This is so critical to your success that it needs to be part of every piece of copywriting you ever create. If you don't, you can kiss your chances of sales goodbye.

So what is the difference between a benefit and a feature? In advertising, features are attributes of the product and benefits are what your customer will actually be getting out of the product. Any feature should have a corresponding benefit or it is just wasted space.

Product: At-home workout program
Feature: 20 workout plans
End Result/Benefit: A muscular, lean body without guessing what exercises to do!

Product: Men's shorts
Feature: Two front zipper pockets
End Result/Benefit: Secure your valuables

Comfort

Security

Elastic waistband with internal drawstring for maximum comfort

Two front zipper pockets, deep enough to secure your valuables

Faux front fly for a more formal look

Soft and stretchy, our signature fabric blend offers comfort and durability

Appearance

Comfort & Quality

Features are great but it's the benefit they offer that we really pay for.

Chapter Summary

- Sell the benefits, not the features.

Good Copy Isn't about Talent

*"The difference between ordinary and extraordinary is
that little extra."*

—Jimmy Johnson

In 2018 I was part of a huge affiliate product launch. I had done
all the basics. I made an insane bonus offer, shared the swipe copy,
hosted the webinars—the "i"s were dotted and the "t"s were
crossed.

The cart opened on a Sunday at midnight. I woke up Monday
morning and went straight to my phone to check the sales. 10
sales . . .

Decent, but underwhelming given the size of my audience.
Then I checked my email and saw the leaderboard from the affiliate program manager, I was in fourth place.

Two of the names above me, I wasn't shocked were there. They
had audiences about the same size as mine, and I knew they'd do
well. But someone else was above me. Someone I knew had maybe
one quarter of my reach. This person was outselling me big time.
Now I am friends with this person and respect their writing tremendously, but I was shocked. It was a wake-up call. I officially
realized that I had let my foot off the gas on my copywriting. It
was time for a hard reset.

When I first started selling things online, I was basically Gary
Halpert and David Ogilvy's love child. I was good, and I worked

hard to make up for any lack of experience I had. I knew less than I know now, but my conversion rates were better.

When my lists were small and I was relatively unknown in my space, every word mattered. If they weren't good, I didn't make money. But as my lists grew, I got spoiled. I started to lay off the gas and became mentally lazy. Emphasis on mentally. I've always been a hard worker in terms of raw output, but mentally, I lose focus often. Mental laziness is rampant in entrepreneurs, and I had fallen into it again.

The revenue would go up or stay the same just because the list did, but I had stopped focusing the same amount of effort on being compelling and putting real effort into my copy.

I kept thinking, "I don't need to get long-winded here. That's corny. People don't need me to sell them on everything—the offer speaks for itself. They'll think I'm just some cheesy marketer if I pull out all the persuasion tactics.

Well, the offer doesn't always speak for itself. At least not to enough people for you to rely on it. Just relying on the value of the offer and assuming the readers will see it and act logically will lead to stagnate sales. The worst part is that you'll still make sales so you might not even notice you're slacking.

It wasn't just my sales emails that I was slacking on either. It was everything. My posts on social media stopped being catchy and interesting. On my YouTube videos, I'd just whip them out and figured people would watch because I knew they were good. I didn't have a hook or any incentive to watch, subscribe, or comment. When I'd share one of my new blog posts, I would say little more than "Hey, go check this out."

Hell, I knew the content was good, so they would too! Right?

I was scatterbrained. I focused on chasing the next biggest thing that was easy to promote versus putting in the work to sell the things I really believed in. To make matters worse, I'd then had the audacity to be annoyed when my results plateaued. Talk about a recipe for building resentment against my industry!

Here is what you can take away from this:

1. Copywriting is just as much (if not more so) about effort than skill.

The odds are great that you're a much better copywriter than you think. Yes, you can and should immerse yourself in the craft, but everyone can be a better copywriter immediately with more effort and awareness.

2. Stop bouncing from one shiny object to another.

It's very likely that you haven't really given the things you're doing now the chance they deserve. So many products and creations I've promoted over the years surely could have done better if I had given them more than one email, one post, one week of attention, etc.

3. More of less is better than less of more.

This is my own Yogi Berra-esque quote, but it makes sense. Go hard on fewer things. Whether that's affiliate products, niches, or business ideas.

Here are some closing tips about copywriting and effort.

Tip 1. Get a copy buddy and review each other's work.

Get a partner and team up. Review each other's work and go beyond just basic spelling and grammar. Look critically at the copy aspect.

Tip 2. Spend more time on everything you promote.

Simple but effective. Stop rushing things. Remind yourself that every first draft could be a better second draft. Step away from your work before you share it and come back with a clear head.

Tip 3. Find creative inspiration from the greats.

Make the habit of noting what grabs your attention and why. When you see great sales copy, ask yourself, "Would this work with my audience? If so, how can I apply it?"

Tip 4. Use the tools available.

Now I'm not a huge fan of cookie cutter sales copy, BUT there are a lot of tools out there that can help you head in the right direction.

Chapter Summary

- Most poor copywriting is a result of laziness rather than a lack of knowledge.
- Don't write on autopilot.

Riddle It with Bullets: Getting the Most Out of the Small

Bullet points are a critical yet often underutilized element of creating sales copy that converts. Bullet points allow you to make your sales copy easier to read and can help you draw attention to the best aspects of your offer.

We are in an increasingly competitive battle for our reader's attention, and bullet points help us make sure visitors have a better understanding of our offer before they decide to leave the page. Using bullet points properly helps reduce the mortal copywriting sin of losing potential customers because we confused or bored them.

A sales page without bullet points is like a face without eyebrows. It just doesn't look right AND it's harder to decipher what someone (sans eyebrows) is saying. Eyebrows are an important part of communicating emotions, just like bullet points are key to communicating benefits.

The following are best practices for crafting and using bullet points in your sales copy. As with all rules, they can be broken, but you need to understand them before you can venture into bending them.

1. Keep Your Bullet Points Short

Remember, the point of bullet points is to quickly make your point. Yes, you can expand on your bullets, but be careful not to overdo it. As a rule of thumb, try to keep your bullet points shorter than a tweet.

If you want to be a rebel and expand on bullet points, do something to make the most important part (the first sentence) stand out from the rest of the text. This can be done with a simple bold, contrasting color, highlights, a different font, or by using ALL CAPS.

2. Keep Your Bullet Points Symmetrical

Great copywriting isn't just about the words used; it's also about how we position the words on the page. Symmetry in our copy refers to the structure and length of our bullet points and how we place them within the sales page.

One piece of symmetry is bullet point length. If your first bullet is 30 characters, it will look goofy if your next bullet is 200 and the one after that is 20. Will it cause you reader to vomit and leave your page in disgust? No, but it will not help your chances of getting your reader to your call to action.

Now don't sacrifice substance and clarity for structure, but when you have 105 bullet points to choose from (more on that in a minute), you should be able to make the bullets aesthetically appealing. Aesthetic appeal doesn't sell products, but it does help us keep the reader on the page so we can get them to read the content that does.

Another aspect of symmetry is how we group our bullet points together. It is highly recommended that you try to use three to five different sets of bullet points spread out evenly throughout any sales page. This seems to be the golden number.

Instead of having fifty bullets in a row, I would break that up into five different lists of ten bullets each, using different bullet types in each of those sections of your copy, and breaking that up with different subsections of your copy and paragraphs so the flow stays even.

Spread your bulleted lists as evenly throughout your sales copy as possible. Don't sacrifice relevance for perfect balance, but you should strive to keep a nice flow to how you break up content with bulleted lists.

Bullet Points

The image above is just a broad example, and your own sales copy may have additional elements like testimonials, videos, etc. Aim to balance your elements accordingly so that the reader doesn't get bored.

3. Bullet Points Don't Have to Be Full Sentences

Don't get caught up on making your bullet points complete sentences. This isn't a fourth grade English class. Get the point across and forget the formalities. Spelling always matters, but you can have sentence fragments, use slang, and bend any rule that makes your bullet points easier for your reader to digest.

Your bank statement is your new report card.

4. Bullet Points Can Be Numbers

It's not the symbol that sells, it's the substance. The structure is what helps draw attention to the substance, so use whatever symbol or number helps draw the reader's attention best. There are actually four ways to create bullets.

- Default "circle" bullets. These are what come to mind when you hear "bullet points" I'm sure.
- Custom icons. You can use unique icons that give even more clarity to your bulleted points. Site builders like Clickfunnels and Thrive Themes make this easy.
- Numbers.
- Custom images. This is a very unique method that can have the same impact as a bulleted list when done properly.

Some may argue that the image above isn't technically a bulleted list, but I say, "Who cares?" It has the exact same impact as a bulleted list. It draws the reader's eye, breaks up monotony, and quickly highlights important features and benefits.

5. Write More Bullets than You Use

My copywriting starts with bullet points. I sit down and write out as many as I can possibly think of. I'll take a break and then write more. I want to end up with many more to choose from than I'll ever use on any sales page.

Your final copy will obviously start with a headline, but a great way to craft a headline is also to start with the bullet points. Doing this will help you realize everything the product has to offer, and you can use this newfound awareness to craft a headline that crushes.

6. Lists of Three Points Are Ideal in Emails and at the End of Sales Pages

Three seems to be the perfect number for bullet points within email marketing campaigns because it allows you to make your point without getting too long winded. Studies show that readers tend to prefer groups of three and are more likely to read them all compared to longer lists. Using just two bullet points looks odd because we are taught in school that bullets should only be used for lists of three or more items. Even though sales copy bends the rules of traditional grammar and formatting, this is one rule I always abide by.

Chapter Summary

- People no longer read every word of a web page; they skim it. Bullet points are the ultimate tool for creating highly skimmable content.
- Brainstorm bullet point ideas and write many more than you actually need. Narrow down to the best ones and use them in your copy.
- Be sure to download the bullet point worksheet at https://evergreenaffiliatemarketing.com/downloads.

Never Look Like an Ad

The average person is now estimated to encounter between 6,000 to 10,000 ads every single day.[15] Constant reminders to buy, try, switch, start, stop, return, and any other of an endless number of calls to action. So much action, it's exhausting just saying no to it.

Blank space is becoming a rare commodity. If our attention is drawn to something, someone will eventually put an ad there or, usually, already has.

If ads weren't such a recent development (relatively speaking compared to our time on the planet), a natural aversion to them would be hardwired into our DNA through evolution.

We are all suffering from ad exhaustion. When something looks like an ad, we tune out. It's not that we hate advertising either, we hate bad advertising. So do yourself and your customer a favor and stop posturing everything as an advertisement, even if it's selling something.

Legendary ad man David Ogilvy wrote, "There is no law which says that advertisements have to look like advertisements. If you make them look like editorial pages, you will attract more readers. Roughly six times as many people read the average article

---

15   Sam Carr, "How Many Ads Do We See a Day in 2021?" PPC Protect, February 15, 2021, https://ppcprotect.com/how-many-ads-do-we-see-a-day.

as the average advertisement. Very few advertisements are read by more than one reader in twenty."[16]

"But where does the selling happen?" you're surely wondering (hopefully in your head and not out loud if you're reading this in a public place).

Maria Veloso answers this question best in her book *Web Copy That Sells*. She explains that selling "comes from expertly crafted copy that tilts the website visitor's favor toward your product or service." She goes on to say, "Avoid blatant sales pitches; instead, provide irresistible information that slides smoothly into a sales pitch for your product."[17]

70:30 Ratio for Advertorial Content

Advertorials are advertisements that are nested inside of regular pieces of content. These aren't the same as ads, but the content is created with the intention of promoting the product in the same way that an ad would.

You see them everywhere, you just might not always recognize them. If you didn't realize you read one, that usually means the creator did a great job with it.

Advertorials are used by many different businesses, and they can work like gangbusters for affiliates as well. This is especially true for affiliates who are running paid ads to content natively. Instead of sending visitors to a sales page, they can send them to something of value that also serves a sales purpose worth paying for.

No one likes a sales letter disguised as a piece of helpful content. To make great advertorial content (on our own platforms or

16   David Ogilvy, *Ogilvy on Advertising* (New York: Penguin, 1985), 129.
17 Maria Veloso, *Web Copy That Sells: The Revolutionary Formula for Creating Killer Copy That Grabs Their Attention and Compels Them to Buy* (New York: AMACOM, 2013), 5.

as guest publications elsewhere) you need to make sure the content is rock solid and that the sales part of the content takes up no more than 30% of the piece.

Great advertorial = 70% Amazing Content + 30% Relevant Product Promotion

Ask yourself, "Is this so helpful that people won't care at all that it is obviously selling something as well?" To make this work, you need to nail the 70:30 ratio and put the content at the forefront.

Chapter Summary

- The best ads don't look like ads.
- The average person is flooded with ads every day. Separate yourself from the majority by creating ads that don't come off as huge sales pitches.
- Advertorials work extremely well for affiliate marketers as long as they focus first on value and second on making sales.

Know More, Sell More

We discussed how it's impossible to promote a massive amount of products with great success. One of the reasons is because if you promote a lot, you need to know a lot.

The more you understand a product that you're promoting, the easier it will be for you to sell it. Your sales copy will flow more smoothly. You'll be able to answer customer questions promptly and accurately (making you look like a rock star), and things are just easier!

Also, if you know what you're promoting inside and out, it makes it extremely easy to create content around it. You can showcase how something works or demonstrate the results you achieved by using it.

This is not to say that you can only promote products that you're currently using. I know this sounds sketchy, but hear me out . . .

If you only promote the tools you're currently using, you could be leading your customers in the wrong direction. For example, my business is at scale. The tools I use such as internet hosting and keyword research software are expensive but very much worth it to me. Many of my readers are brand new to affiliate marketing, and if I were to recommend just the high end products I use, I'd be causing them to waste money and bring a gun to a knife fight, so to speak.

So I go out of my way to master the alternatives if I need to recommend them. If it's a product, I buy it, even if I already have a different higher-end solution. If it's a service, I test it. Dive deep into all the features and benefits. Explore all of the possible uses.

You get the idea. Whether you use it or not, get to know it before you promote it. It will benefit not only your customers but your sales as well.

Chapter Summary

- Know the products you promote inside and out.
- Dive deep into all of the features, benefits, and potential uses of the products you promote so you can answer questions effectively and create more compelling sales copy.

Beat the Buzzer

Scarcity is like steroids for product launches. If you're promoting something that is time sensitive, you can and should use this to your advantage. One thing you'll notice when promoting a product with scarcity (time or quantity) is that as the product nears its end, conversions go through the roof.

I've found that on large launches the norm is about 50% of all sales come in the last twenty-four hours. Likewise, the last 20% of a product with a quantity limit (e.g., only 100 licenses left at this price) see conversion rates boosted by 200% or more.

Use this to your advantage. If a particular offer is a large part of your yearly income, don't be afraid to really go hard as you near the finish line. This means multiple emails, live events, etc. Anything that can get eyeballs on the offer during this small window of time that sees massive conversion boosts.

Chapter Summary

- When promoting something with scarcity, almost 50% of the sales will come on the final day.
- Be aggressive on the last day and don't be shy about promoting very intensely.

The Rule of Seven

Remember the myth that you can just post a link and get paid? Part of why that rarely works is because of what advertisers know as the "Rule of Seven." It is a rule of thumb that states that prospective buyers need to hear the marketing message at least seven times before they actually buy it from you.

This is an old rule, and I believe that with the rising cost of attention online, the number is significantly higher now. It may be closer to twice this now (fourteen impressions). The exact number isn't as important as the underlying concept that people need to be exposed to your marketing much more than you probably think.

The number of impressions needed is also going to vary with the price of the item you're selling. In his book *Invisible Selling Machine*, Ryan Deiss explains this well.

> "You don't need to kill an ant with an atom bomb. You don't need a 30 day email series to sell a low-dollar product. If it's been 3–5 days and they haven't bought —it's okay. . . . Start talking to them about another topic."[18]

If you run paid ads, we measure this in "frequency." Many advertisers will turn off their advertising if their frequency reaches a

---

18   Ryan Deiss, *Invisible Selling Machine* (Digital Marketing Lab, 2015), 58.

number that they deem to be too high. More often than not, the number is far below the actual number that is most effective.

When I first started running paid ads, I'd panic at the sight of a frequency over 3.0 (meaning the average person in the advertising group had seen the ad three times). Now, I'm more than comfortable going above this number.

Keep in mind, this doesn't mean that you should run the same advert more than seven times to your audience. You can (and should) be running different ads for the same product. If someone can see seven different ads for your product, you're well on the way to getting the maximum number of sales from that group as possible. Of course, the total sales you make is relative to the quality of the ad, product, market fit, etc. Following the Rule of Seven will merely ensure that you give everything the best possible chance to succeed. It won't fix bad advertising, but it will give you a fair picture of how effective or ineffective your advertising is.

Remember, this Rule of Seven doesn't need to be limited to paid advertising either. Getting "impressions" can come in many forms.

- a blog post that mentions the product organically
- a podcast episode that mentions the product in the trailer
- an email promoting the product
- you doing a live video wearing merchandise from the product

Get creative with your impressions, but do be sure to actually make them happen. Most marketers are not seeing the conversion rates they could be because they aren't maximizing exposure. They assume that since someone saw something and didn't buy immediately, they aren't interested. This is wrong.

- They might have been on mobile and wanted to buy later when they got to their desktop.
- They might have wanted to check out a competitor first.
- They might have been waiting for a check to clear before they bought anything with their card.
- They might have had a banking issue and needed to circle back.

The list of reasons is endless. Don't assume that someone will never buy something just because they didn't buy immediately. Use the Rule of Seven as a minimum. When in doubt, err on the side of overexposure as long as you don't diminish the value of your content.

One of the podcasts I listen to regularly does this extremely well. At first, I was scratching my head wondering why on earth they were promoting the same product over and over at the beginning of their show. It made perfect sense, though, once I remembered the Rule of Seven. Their subtle plug at the beginning of what was at least 100 episodes made their affiliate product top-of-mind. Also, since it was a podcast, they also benefited from repeatedly sharing their special offer code. I could go to the site and enter it by memory now, and I haven't heard the ad in quite a while.

Chapter Summary

- The Rule of Seven is the idea that consumers need to be exposed to a product on average seven times before they are ready to buy.
- Mentioning something one time is not enough to truly maximize your conversions.
- Focus on regularly mentioning your affiliate offers, especially your cornerstone offer.

Testing the Right Way

"Never stop testing, and your advertising will never stop improving."

—David Ogilvy

This quote is so powerful that I've chosen to include it twice in this book. Doing something once and assuming it is perfect out of the gate is like a child swinging a baseball bat for the first time and expecting it to remain the same for their entire lifetime. Even if your results are fantastic, your first work will never be the best it can be.

A headline that gets higher than average click throughs could easily see an improvement by changing a single word. A YouTube video that seemed like a failure can be revived with a simple change of your thumbnail graphic.

This holds true with anything you create. For example, in the nineteenth century Guy de Maupassant changed the title of his book *The Tallow Ball to A French Prostitute's Sacrifice* and sales went from 15,000 to 54,700.[19]

When it comes to testing, there are two types that affiliate

---

19   "Examples of Books that Took Off When the Publisher Changed the Titles," Writing for a Living, November 2, 2017, https://writingforaliving.us/2017/11/02/examples-books-took-off-publisher-changed-titles.

marketers use. They are A/B testing and multi-variate testing. There are many third-party tools that make this possible.

Multivariate tests compare several versions of a webpage with multiple different elements to see how those elements interact as a whole and how they impact your conversions, clicks, or whatever metric you're measuring. Multivariate tests try to find what combination of elements is most likely to achieve your objectives.

Multivariate Testing

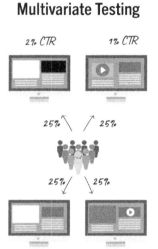

A/B split testing is not as complex as multivariate testing. A/B testing looks at two versions of a webpage with one difference between them. The original version of a webpage (the control) is compared against a variation with only one element changed. Using the various tools at our disposal, we send a percentage of traffic to one variant and the rest to the other. Typically, this is a 50/50 split, but that number can vary.

A/B Testing

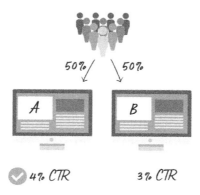

50% / \ 50%

A   *B*

✅ 4% CTR   3% CTR

The benefit of A/B testing is that we know exactly which elements made the most meaningful changes. With multivariate testing, we can't as easily pinpoint exactly which elements had the biggest impact. If each variant has five different elements, the combination that performs the best may have three elements that perform above average and two that perform below average. We can't identify exactly which are which, so we take the results holistically.

My favorite approach is to start with multivariate testing to find a winner of several broad tests and then A/B test individual elements of the winning variants. Whichever approach you take, as long as you obey the following rules, you'll see consistent results.

Rule 1. Never Stop Testing

In a perfect world, we'd test everything. Unfortunately, we don't have that kind of time. We have to prioritize the things that are of the highest value. For example, the title of your highest performing blog post or the display of your core lead magnets.

Although we can't test everything, we can and should test

relentlessly. If you don't have a test running at any given time, you're missing out on a chance for improvement.

Rule 2. Wait for Statistical Significance

Be patient with your testing. I'm a huge baseball fan, so I'm going to draw on it to demonstrate this. Great managers work hard to find ideal matchups between hitters and pitchers. If a rookie came into the big leagues and homered off of a Cy Young Award–winning pitcher, it would be irrational to assume that going forward, the batter will continue to hit that pitcher well.

To make a reasonable decision, the manager needs to wait until there is statistical significance. This means enough at bats to gauge whether or not the first at bat was an outlier or there is a true advantage for the hitter.

This is how we need to approach our testing. If we split a test 50/50 and 100 visits go to page A and 100 visits go to site B, we won't have nearly enough data to make a good decision. With only 100 visits each, a few conversions could skew the results significantly. With 1,000+ visits to each page, we will start to see more reliable data that we can start to trust more. The larger the sample, the more reliable the results will be.

Rule 3. A/B Test One Element at a Time

Unlike multi-variate testing, A/B testing requires us to test one element at a time. We cannot move on to the next element until we've found a winner of the first test. Failing to do this will dilute our results.

Rule 4. Prioritize A/B Elements

Although every aspect of whatever you are testing matters, not every element is created equal. Your headline or title, for example, will always be the most important element. So you won't start by testing text font sizes or color. You start with the headline and work down. On sales or landing pages, you'll want to start from the top down after you've completed a multi-variate test.

I prioritize two things and the rest can vary based on how easy they are to implement or how confident you are they will make a meaningful change. The first thing I test is the headline. For search engine type content, this is the title as it appears in search results. For landing pages that I send traffic to directly, this is the main headline.

Next, I test the call to action. Inside the call to action, there are multiple elements worth testing, including the actual call to action text (such as "Click here to get started for free") and the call to action style (color, display, sub-headline).

Chapter Summary

- Test relentlessly. You should have some sort of test going at every moment.
- Prioritize the elements you test and start with the most important and work down.
- Wait for statistical significance before choosing winning variations.

MISCELLANEOUS THOUGHTS AND CONSIDERATIONS

Retention Matters

The best affiliate marketers understand that earning more is not just about driving more sales. It's about maximizing the LTV (lifetime value) of each sale they make. Studies have shown that on average, it costs nearly five times as much to acquire a new customer as it does to keep an existing one.[20] This applies just as much to affiliate marketing as it does with any other business model. Whether it's reducing refunds on one-time purchases or reducing churn rate and cancellations on recurring subscriptions, we win when our referrals enjoy and use what we refer to them.

The best way to do this is to make sure that you do everything in your power to make the referral get maximum value from the product. We can do this in three main ways.

- help educate the buyer
- help with support
- add value to the purchase

Educating the buyer on how to get the most out of what they've purchased will dramatically decrease refunds. Although creating training type content isn't going to drive a ton of sales (people

---

20 Will Tidey, "Acquisition vs. Retention: The Importance of Customer Lifetime Value," Huify, February 17, 20018, https://www.huify.com/blog/acquisition-vs-retention-customer-lifetime-value.

who need training on something usually already own said product), it is going to help you with retention.

Create content that shows your followers how to get the most out of the things you recommend. Show demos or quick tips that help guide them in the right direction. If you are able to get a list of the buyers, send them this content and help them get value fast. This is especially true for your cornerstone affiliate products.

When it comes to helping after the sale, we should be involved with the support if needed. Although one of the perks of affiliate marketing is that you have to provide less customer support, that doesn't mean you should be completely hands off. If someone emails you asking about a product that you referred them to, reply.

Finally, we can reduce refunds by adding additional value to anyone who purchases from us. If you make the purchase more valuable by adding something to it, you'll make the cancellation and refunds fall to the floor. I covered this more in the chapter about adding bonuses to your offers to boost conversions.

Remember, the sale isn't done just because money has exchanged hands. Treat retention the same way you treat conversions.

Chapter Summary

- Helping decrease refunds or cancellations can't be overlooked. Keeping customers is easier than getting new ones.
- We can reduce refunds and churn rate in three main ways: (1) help educate the buyer, (2) help with support after the sale, and (3) add value to the purchase.

The Truth about Running Paid Ads

If you're a new affiliate marketer, you have surely considered running paid ads directly to your affiliate products. Ranking on page 1 of Google or going viral on social media organically is hard, so it's extremely tempting to buy your way out of the work.

You're not alone. I did this too several years ago when I got started in the business. My results were . . . underwhelming.

We were under the impression that we didn't need a brand to sell affiliate products. We assumed that we could sell ANY product simply by running paid traffic to the landing pages of our affiliates, optimizing the ads, scaling them, and pretty much printing our own money.

This was a total failure. It was extremely disappointing because the numbers had added up perfectly on paper.

For example, let's say that you have a product that has a $2.18 EPC according to the affiliate network or vendor. EPC means that for each click, you should be earning $2.18. Based on this, you'd expect that you could easily profit as long as your costs per click are below that $2.18.

For example.
- spend $.75 on a click, net $1.43
- spend $.18 on a click, net $2
- spend $2 on a click, net $.18

Seems to make sense, but here is why it doesn't work.

1. Affiliate Vendors Aren't Consistent in What "EPC" Means

Some affiliate networks measure their EPC differently. A few of the large platforms measure their EPC as "Earnings per 100 Clicks." Unfortunately, they don't label it as earnings per 100 clicks (EPHC)—they like to keep it confusing. They do this because it makes their available affiliate products look more enticing to potential promoters.

So if you've been running ads to an affiliate that has EPC measured as EPHC (earnings per hundred clicks), your ad costs per click need to be measured accordingly.

If you're paying $.30/click and the EPHC is $20.00, you're losing money. You'd need to convert your EPC to EPHC or vice versa. You need to measure them with the same unit. So if you decided to convert your ad costs into EPHC, you'd need to multiply by 100. This means you're actually paying $30 EPHC.

$30 for 100 clicks will mean you're losing $10 because the average EPHC is only $20.

$20 earned − $30 spent = −$10

Instead of a money printing press, you've created a money shredder. This is, of course, assuming that the EPHC is an accurate reflection of potential earnings (it sometimes is not). Always verify what EPC actually means for each site.

If you don't check, you may not even know this until it's way too late.

2. EPC Represents All Traffic Sources, Not Cold Traffic

The EPC is calculated based on all clicks and sales and it doesn't break down the costs in terms of traffic. For example, if the EPC is $5, cold traffic will not get an EPC of $5. This is because cold traffic will always convert at lower rates, which means it costs more. The $5 EPC weighs the hot traffic and the cold traffic together. Some traffic will earn far more than $5 EPC and some will earn far less.

Here are the six big problems you'll run into when running paid traffic to affiliate offers.

Problem 1. Conversion Tracking Limitations

Although it's becoming more common with software like Thrive-Cart adding the ability to let affiliates add their conversion codes to third-party websites, it's still very rare. Successful campaigns need great metrics and deep analysis.

As Peter Drucker wisely said, "What gets measured gets managed."

Since we can't directly track all conversions, we can't be 100% positive how well our ads are performing. We don't own the sites for the products we promote, so we can't just add our code to confirmation pages, abandoned carts, etc.

Since we can't directly track all conversions, we can't be 100% positive how well our ads are performing.

Problem 2. Social Media Platform Limitations

Not every social media platform is affiliate friendly. Research the terms and conditions of any platform that you're considering using and ensure that running direct ads to affiliate offers is allowed. The last thing that you want is to have an ad account banned for an easily avoidable mistake.

Problem 3. Clicks Can Be Hard to Scale

This isn't the biggest hold up here, but it is a hold up. The more clicks you want, the higher the costs will be and the broader you'll have to make the audience in order to get them. So if the product is very niche-specific and the audience is small, clicks can be difficult to come by on a long-term basis.

There are plenty of tricks to get more clicks on your ads, but it can still be difficult to scale these sorts of campaigns.

Problem 4. Traffic Needs to Be Warmed Up

If you take one thing from this chapter, it should be that warming your traffic always leads to more sales. If you don't provide some sort of value up front, you shouldn't be surprised that you aren't making sales.

Paid ads to affiliate products shown to cold traffic fail in large part because there is no trust built or value previously given. The folks at digitalmarketer.com put it well and compare selling to cold traffic to proposing to someone on your first date. She might say yes, but that would be very unlikely and you're going to look weird.

The affiliate product I mentioned at the beginning of the chapter that had a $2.18 EPC is the average of all traffic. Most of that traffic is warm and sent by affiliates who have already built trust with their followers. The EPC provided by major affiliate platforms is an average of cold, warm, and hot traffic. If you're sending cold traffic to an affiliate page, you will almost always get a lower EPC than the average that is provided by the affiliate network.

Problem 5. Succeeding with Paid Traffic Takes Practice

The "direct to affiliate link" paid ad approach is a common attraction to new marketers who haven't created very many ads for anything prior. Although it's always difficult to pull off these direct-to-affiliate offer promotions, it's extremely difficult if you don't understand how to make a quality, targeted ad with compelling sales copy.

Problem 6. Good Ads Aren't "Hands Off"

The dream of creating one ad for an affiliate product and "setting it and forgetting it" while you rake in commissions is just that, a dream. In reality, most ads need tweaking periodically to maintain high CTRs (click through rates). If you keep targeting the same users, they will develop "banner blindness" and will stop engaging with your ad.

Okay, we've gone through the problems, here are the solutions to make paid traffic work for you.

1. Send to Your Own Content First

This is where the sexiness disappears but the effectiveness shows up. You should send your traffic to a blog post, YouTube video, webinar, or anything else that can provide some sort of value and more than just pitch a product. The affiliate product should tie seamlessly into the sale of the product.

Providing value before the sale is extremely important. Dr. Robert Cialdini, author of the best seller *Influence: The Psychology of Persuasion*, performed many studies around the concept of reciprocity and why giving something away often leads to getting more in return later.

Caildini performed a case study in which a waiter's tips increased by 3% when diners are given a mint, and 14% when they're given two mints. When the waiter left one mint with the bill but quickly returned to offer a second mint, the tips increased to 23%.[21]

It's not guesswork. Providing value FIRST will make you more money as an affiliate in the long run. This is part of why the anonymous approach rarely outperforms creating a brand and providing value for "free" to the masses.

This is part of why I have spent so much time writing this book. Although I make money on the book sales, the real earning potential for me comes through the fact that by giving you value, you're more likely to support me later if I promote something.

---

21   Robert Cialdini, *Influence: The Psychology of Persuasion* (New York: Harper-Collins, 2007) 32.

Sorry if that makes you feel like you're being played. You're of course perfectly welcome to scour my blog and YouTube channel and absorb every bit of free information without ever giving me a dollar.

There are additional positive byproducts of running paid traffic to your own content as well. If you have a blog or video channel, you can start to rank organically if users are viewing the content, liking, commenting, and sharing. This means more free traffic over time, which will lead to more sales even if you stop running the ads.

Another positive byproduct of sending traffic to your own content is you can capture email addresses if you include an enticing lead magnet somewhere on your page or channel.

2. Pixel Traffic and Retarget It

The purpose of sending traffic to content that isn't just a sales page is because it warms the traffic. Warm traffic buys.

Pixeling traffic allows you to retarget past visitors to your page and show additional ads to them as they navigate across the internet. This is absolutely the best traffic you can target.

- They know you and are more likely to trust your future recommendations.
- They are more likely to be interested in what you're selling.
- It takes out a lot of the guesswork of creating an audience from scratch.
- People rarely purchase anything the first time they are exposed to it.
- If someone has received value from you in the past, they are much more likely to click on an ad you show them later, and they are more likely to buy as well.

3. Continually Optimize

The higher your frequency gets, the more money you're going to pay per click. This means that we need to make sure we don't fall victim to "setting and forgetting" our ads.

Now a slight exception is when you are running ads to just pixeled traffic. If you are targeting recent visitors to your site, you won't need to change the ad quite as often since new visitors will be pixeled each day, and they will be seeing your ads for the first time.

4. Collect Emails When Possible

If you're spending money on ads, you may as well grab some emails as a byproduct. When you gather email addresses, you can contact your subscribers again later with offers to your affiliate products.

5. Sell in Email Follow-Up Sequences

New email subscribers are giving you the chance to expose them to your offer multiple times. Create a great follow-up campaign that builds trust and gives incentive to buy and you'll see your sales go much, much higher.

6. Test Multiple Ad Platforms

Some products sell better on certain mediums. Test as many as you can and double down on what works for you.

Chapter Summary

- Paid ads absolutely work for affiliate marketing, but they aren't for everyone.
- You need to be prepared to spend a good deal of money up front just to gather information to optimize your ads.

- Try to collect emails with your ads whenever possible and sell in automated follow ups.
- Test like crazy. Test different platforms, media types, audiences, and budgets.
- Pixel everything when possible for retargeting. Retargeting ads will almost always see lower costs and higher conversion rates.

Handling Negativity

Affiliate marketing is a unique industry in terms of its polarity. Many people dislike affiliate marketers and the process in general. Remember how I said affiliate marketing has a checkered past? Well, it's created a lot of negative energy in the space and we all have to carry the weight of it.

Be careful, though, in how you choose to handle this inevitable push back. How you choose to respond or not respond to criticism, trolls, or "haters" matters more than you may think.

I used to reply back to "haters" in the comments of my content and tell myself, "They weren't going to like me or buy what I have to sell anyway . . . Who cares." However, that's far from the case. How we choose to reply is a showcase of our character and personality to everyone watching. People who respect us are watching. People who dislike us are watching. How do we want them to see us?

Also, we live in a "screenshot and share" age where even an email thread can become a public showcase of how well or poorly you handle criticism if someone decides to share it with others. If they really don't like you, that's very likely!

The knee-jerk reaction to someone saying something negative about you or your business is to label them a "troll" or a "hater." As great as it is to turn away and just say, "Oh forget that person, they're just hating on me for no reason," it isn't a one-size-fits-all solution. It's an example of cognitive dissonance. We don't want to accept (let alone consider) that we've possibly acted out of line with how we want to portray ourselves, so we quickly find an answer to why someone is saying we did.

"This is tacky!" "This is a money grab!" "The audio on this video is garbage!" etc., etc. We want to quickly dispel the way these sorts of comments make us feel. So we slap the "hater" label on and move on with our day. But what if we are being tacky? Wouldn't you like to change that? This could be that chance!

What if you did fall into a promotion that comes off as a quick money grab. Wouldn't you want to consider that maybe you're actually harming your reputation since others might feel that way too? Isn't it worth at least considering it? What if your audio IS bad (it probably is, I'm speaking from experience here). Wouldn't you like to fix it?

Quickly labeling negative comments as hate is a very mentally lazy approach and a missed opportunity for growth. Yes, that means a little bit of pain and ego-deflation, but we all know how it goes: "No pain, no gain." Yes, we need to know the difference between constructive feedback and flat-out mean-spirited hate, but it's often far less clear than it appears on the surface.

Many of the people who say negative things aren't actually haters. Lots of the time there is actually some truth to what they say, regardless to how aggressively they decided to deliver it. Back in those early days, I should have taken more inward reflections after experiencing these "haters" rather than writing them off (the easy way).

If someone is insulting your looks or things you can't control, ignore them and move on. I know this is much easier said than done, but the thickness of your skin can be the X factor to how far you're willing to go in business.

"There is only one way to avoid criticism: Do nothing, say nothing, and be nothing."

—Aristotle

I take a lot of action. All successful entrepreneurs do. Lots of action means lots of mistakes. Sometimes, they can be pretty big ones.

A mistake doesn't define your character. So why is it that we feel so bothered when we have to face up to them? We understand that they're an inevitable byproduct of the process. By shifting perspective, we can learn to deal with them gracefully.

"Hater Math": Letting a handful of negative remarks outweigh exponentially more positive ones. We tend to focus on the negative much more and 1 negative comment can have a more noticeable impact on us than 1,000 positive ones. Don't fall into this.

Hater Math

Do I really think I'm perfect? How narcissistic would that be? If I'm not perfect, does that change my underlying character? Of course not. So why would I beat myself up too much for something that is inevitably a part of life?

If someone says something about me that I know isn't true, I should brush it off without dwelling on it. If their criticism is true, it should be addressed on my end, corrected, and then left in the past where it belongs. Mistakes happen, it's our character that we should be concerned with.

Chapter Summary

- It takes thick skin to make it in the affiliate marketing space.
- Don't write off all negative comments as "haters." Often there is a valuable lesson we can learn, even if it was shared in a rude or condescending way.
- Don't let the few negative comments blind you from all of the positive ones.

Hire Help

You are a business. Even if your affiliate marketing revolves around your personality and brand, you are a business. A business thrives with help, and an affiliate marketing business is no different.

Please, never confuse working for yourself with working by yourself. Outsourcing can help you grow your business exponentially faster, but it's far from easy. There's a reason not everyone does it. It's so much harder than it looks.

Tell me if this sounds familiar (and it doesn't have to be related to business). You've tried to get someone to do a job for you but ended up doing it yourself because it was harder to explain it than just do it yourself. This is one of the greatest killers of proper outsourcing.

At first, you should be able to do something faster and better. In fact, you might never be able to hire someone to do a task as well as you'd like it done. That doesn't mean you shouldn't outsource it out.

We're all cursed with the limitation of time. In internet business, you're going to constantly chase the dragon of "enough" or "everything is finished." There is no such thing as done. If you create content, you could always create more. If you run paid ads, you could always optimize them more. If you do webinars, you could always do more. You get the picture.

The key is to identify the tasks that are the highest value to you. The things that you do better than others AND that make you the most ROI for your time and effort. Fill all of your time with these things and outsource the rest.

Reality check, we're not irreplaceable. Not by a long shot. We can always find someone who can do something at least almost as good as we can. Yes, this requires that we fight the urge to micro-manage and let go of some things for the greater good.

So what can affiliate marketers outsource? The answer: almost anything. If you can do it, someone else could be hired to do it as well. With the exception of your own brand and personality, everything else could be delegated away.

Even better, most tasks can be outsourced at wages far lower than you might have imagined to virtual assistants overseas. Now, not everything should be done "on the cheap," but some things, absolutely. Here are some of the biggest things affiliate marketers can delegate to a low-cost virtual assistant (in alphabetical order, not in order of importance of value).

- backlink building
- booking you on shows and podcasts
- bookkeeping
- cold email outreach
- content research
- customer support
- editing videos
- engaging with influencers
- finding affiliate offers
- general research
- graphic design
- managing your schedule
- miscellaneous admin tasks
- optimizing sales copy

- planning launch schedules
- proofreading content
- replying to comments
- repurposing content
- SEO
- web design
- writing blog posts
- writing emails
- and much more!!!

The list doesn't need to be limited to just business tasks either. You can outsource personal tasks as well because that can free up more time to work on the things with higher ROIs to your business.

- paying your bills
- scheduling flights
- sending gifts
- ordering food
- etc., etc.

You don't need to stop at virtual tasks either. You can hire people in your area to do things like:

- childcare
- cleaning the house
- cooking meals
- yard work
- etc., etc.

You get the idea. Anything that you don't love doing that takes away from your highest ROI tasks can be delegated. There are few things as gratifying as knowing that work is getting done behind the scenes without you!

Finding and hiring quality help is a topic that has been covered in 300-page books. I can't do justice to it here, so I'm going to give you the 80:20 really fast.

- **Create SOPs (standard operating procedures) of everything you do in your life and business.** This will make outsourcing much easier. You can give your new hires the SOPs, and they can get started much more quickly.
- **Hire slow and fire fast.** You're going to go through a lot of virtual assistants and freelancers. That's okay. Don't beat yourself up if something doesn't go right. Keep at it and put in the work to make it work.
- **Meet with your team regularly.** Don't let your team be "out of sight and out of mind." Even if they're trustworthy, you want to make sure that you regularly check in and make sure you're all on the same page. Make them feel like part of the business rather than just a paid employee.

Chapter Summary

- Working for yourself doesn't mean you have to work by yourself. Hire help whenever possible.
- Focus on doing what you do best and outsource everything else.
- Hire slow and fire fast, create SOPs, and meet with your freelancers regularly.

Average Joe Commissions

If you've read this far into the book, it's likely that you want to be a serious affiliate marketer and wouldn't mind having "affiliate marketer" as your job title. But what if you want to pursue other things?

Look, I love affiliate marketing, but what I really love is making money on my own terms. If you're like me, you don't want to tie yourself down to labels. If your goal is seeing how far you can push this life and your business, remaining flexible to other opportunities is something you should consider.

Now if you decide to branch into something else, that doesn't mean you can't still reap the benefits of affiliate marketing. There are no rules that say all affiliate marketers have to have a linear focus and can only earn money from commissions. In fact, some of the people I know who have racked up the most commissions aren't traditional affiliate marketers at all.

Once you understand what affiliate marketing is and how it works, you'll start to see ways that anyone could implement it into their businesses. With a little creativity, you can add affiliate offers to your other work or freelance gigs to drive additional revenue or even recurring commissions.

Here's an example. You could create a Fiverr gig titled *"I will help you create a killer lead magnet."* You could charge whatever you want for this, but the real earning potential could come after the sale when you recommend affiliate offers to your clients.

If I were to create a lead magnet for someone, I'd include the following at some point.

> *"Here's the lead magnet. If you like the design, I created this with a cool $27 tool called Designrr. I highly recommend you check it out if you want to create other variations of this lead magnet or make other lead magnets in the future without paying me* 🙂 *. Also, I highly recommend that you check out the ConvertKit autoresponder for getting this lead magnet to your subscribers. It does wonders for my email automations, and I recommend it to all of my clients."*

By doing this I've now referred two affiliate products that are highly relevant to the customer and could lead to additional revenue in one-time or recurring payments. If they purchase ConvertKit, I could be paid monthly indefinitely. This approach makes freelancing much more attractive.

You can do this method on Fiverr or any other freelance marketplace you choose (Upwork, FreeUp, etc.). Just be careful not to come off too salesy. It's a gray hat tactic for marketplaces like Fiverr, but if you do it tactfully and in a way that is helpful and relevant to your customers, you shouldn't have any issues.

Eventually, try to shift away from marketplaces you don't own and sell directly from your own site. This will give you total freedom over what you promote.

Here's another example. You run a digital ad agency. You use a page builder that you believe has better functionality for optimizing for conversions. This means that you can help drive better results for your clients. So you recommend that they purchase the page builder, and they do so with the affiliate link you provide them. You're now making additional revenue for every single customer you bring into your agency.

Chapter Summary

- You don't have to be a traditional affiliate marketer to earn tons of commissions.
- Think about organic opportunities for promoting relevant products to a niche you're already in.

Do It Once with Templates

Affiliate marketing can involve a surprising amount of design work.

- ads
- content thumbnails
- channel art
- animations and GIFs
- miscellaneous graphics

The list goes on and the time required adds up. I wish I could have back just a fraction of the time I've spent over the years making designs. The sad/ironic part is that the designs were usually crap.

The absolute best thing you can do is create a few quality, branded template designs that work and don't overthink the process. I'm not saying that design doesn't matter, but you can get great results by doing it right once and just painting inside the lines going forward.

You can do this yourself, but I highly recommend you get tons of feedback because your design eye will evolve with time. I am disgusted by some of the things I made that I thought were great designs. Getting a core, branded theme (colors, fonts, styles) and some templates that can be easily edited in one minute, not an hour, will give you back the time you should be spending on higher-value tasks and will make your designs convert better.

Also, templates will keep your brand image consistent. Consistency is usually more valuable than overall creativity. A brand that is consistent looks more professional and is more memorable.

If you really want to get off on the right foot (and aren't afraid to spend some money), hire a quality designer to create a brand theme and basic brand assets for you. Typically, you'd start by having a logo created and then build your assets around that.

Be skeptical of cheap designers. Just because someone sells design work, that doesn't mean they are good. Anyone can say they are a professional, but their work will do the real talking.

Chapter Summary

- Stop creating everything from scratch. Save templates of the things you create repeatedly.
- Templates not only save time, but they help you with brand consistency.

One-Time vs. Recurring Payouts

Recurring payments are great, but focusing all your efforts on promoting them you might be leaving money on the table. Here are a few things to keep in mind when considering recurring versus one-time payout structures.

First, you should always promote the best product to your followers regardless of the payout structure. Focusing exclusively on recurring products can damage the real value to your customers if it encourages you to promote something of lesser quality. This is one of the reasons affiliate marketing gets a bad reputation.

Next, keep in mind that recurring affiliate programs are typically more competitive. You aren't the only one who wants the security of recurring payments. This means conversions will be harder to come by in most cases.

Also, recurring product customers have a LTV (LifeTime Value) that is often lower than you might expect. Some affiliate programs might pay you monthly, but that doesn't mean the referral is planning on staying forever. Many recurring plans have short lifetimes, and selling things with yearly or one-time payments can actually lead to far higher LTVs. Most quality affiliate programs will give you a good idea of the average

lifetime value of a conversion. Look at this number as opposed to the more fantastical idea of eternal recurring sales. Everyone cancels everything eventually.

Having assets that drive one-time sales consistently is just as valuable (if not more powerful). I'd rather have a blog post (for example) that drives ten one-time sales per month than have ten recurring subscriptions per month. Yes, both decay (subscribers cancel and content can lose traffic over time if not updated), but we need to view this in relative terms.

Recurring programs are great, but they aren't always better. Focusing on them exclusively can harm your value to your followers, force you to compete with more affiliates, and ironically even lead to less bottom-line earnings for you.

Chapter Summary

- There is a place for both one-time payment and recurring payment affiliate products.
- Promote the best products, regardless of payout structure.
- Consider the LTV (lifetime value) of a sale. Often a one-time payment can be the higher-value option.

High Ticket vs. Low Ticket

This chapter is going to make many of you very, very uncomfortable. You may even be tempted to drop this book where you stand because the advice is very counterintuitive and it is going to go against a lot of what many of the wealthiest affiliate marketers suggest. You will be leaving money on the table if you decide to focus on ethics first and not just on finding the most expensive things you can promote.

Make no mistake about it; it's almost always easier to make more money with high ticket offers that typically come in the form of coaching programs or courses. Every niche has their own version of these, but they are very common in the make money online space.

Making someone pull out their credit card to buy is difficult, regardless of the price point but a $500 to $2,500 commission is far more rewarding than a $50 to $250 one. With few exceptions, it's easier to make massive paydays by promoting high ticket programs throughout the year. But, unfortunately, we don't measure our success in gross profits.

Highlight this: Very few high ticket offers are actually a good fit for your audience. Unfortunately, although we can make large sums of money very quickly, it often requires a high level of selling out.

As someone who has bought and sold high ticket offers (anything over $997 I consider to be high ticket), I can tell you that it's not the best way to truly serve your audience.

High ticket offers aren't always bad. There is truth in the idea that if someone "has skin in the game," they will be far more likely to actually do the work necessary to succeed. I'm much more likely to finish a movie I bought for $10 than I am to finish a free movie from Netflix, for example. Beyond that though, there is almost always a lower cost alternative of equal or greater value to most high ticket offers.

Here are my biggest issues with high ticket offers:

- **Quality is overstated due to an army of highly paid affiliates.** It's easy to buy something when everyone around you is saying it's fantastic, but when there is a lot of money involved, the product isn't usually as good as it seems.
- **Success stories are misleading.** When you have thousands of buyers, there will always be outliers who do extremely well. However, many would have done well anyway. If you take 1,000 people who are serious enough to spend $2,000 to learn X skill, a huge number of them would have succeeded regardless of the high ticket program. This is used as artificial social proof.
- **Price is incorrectly associated with quality.** This is another reason why it's so hard to resist high ticket offers, the conversion rates aren't as different from low ticket offers as you might expect. This is because people incorrectly associate price with quality. They will buy the highest priced product assuming it's a guarantee. How could someone charge that much if it's not the real deal? The answer is, very easily.

So am I completely opposed to high ticket offers? Not entirely, but I truly believe about 99% of things priced over $997 aren't actually the best fit for your audience. Here are things that might make me reconsider if a high ticket program is actually worth a high price point:

- A results-based guarantee. This is almost unheard of. Most programs offer a refund of some kind and it's more of a legal obligation that is used as a sales point, but that's far from the same as a results-based guarantee. If I know that everyone who buys what I promote will get their end result, I'm absolutely in.
- 1 on 1 support. Charging more than $997 for digital-only content simply doesn't fly in 2021. Now if someone offers customized, real-world support to go along with a program, that's something of real value.
- Something of tangible value. Most high ticket programs have little to no real costs beyond advertising. An example of this is the best way to explain what I mean. I purchased a program that taught video editing, and it came with a yearly subscription to a software that I was going to buy anyway that would have cost $597. They included something of unique value to me and at real cost to them.

While they aren't the cash cows that high ticket programs are, small ticket offers (things under $997) have a place in your affiliate marketing business and can help you make money AND keep the best interest of your followers front and center.

Small Ticket Buys Grease the Gears of Trust

Trust is the heart of successful affiliate marketing. By selling helpful products, regardless of the payout, we can build trust. Trust that can lead customers to eventually buy again when we offer a high ticket offer.

Something magical happens when someone pulls out their credit card when we endorse something. Even if the purchase is $1, customers who have bought from us once are much more likely to buy from us again.

Showing them we deliver on small buys makes them exponentially more likely to trust us on larger purchases. For that reason, small ticket offers can help sell big ticket items.

Even if the earnings on the low ticket offer are minimal, the immeasurable value of increasing the odds of them spending more is something we can't overlook.

Small Ticket Offers Can Add Up
Yes, you'll need many more conversions on small ticket offers, but if a product is helpful and relevant, not mentioning it helps no one.

Small Ticket Offers Require Less Focus
Big ticket sales merit a good deal of focus and attention. Small ticket offers can perform very well organically or through passive promotions through automated follow ups or evergreen content.

Small Ticket Offers Can Liquidate Ad Spend
If you're running paid traffic, low ticket offers can accomplish two important things. They can help offset ad spend, and they can help you distinguish the "cream" of the crop. If you're paying $2 for an email opt-in, running a sequence that promotes a small offer (say a $14 e-book) can easily help you offset the ad spend. If you earn just $2 on average per click, you're building your audience for free. Earn more and you are building your audience and getting paid to do it.

Also, if you're unsure of the quality of your opt-ins, low ticket offers will help you to identify the best potential customers. For example, if you purchased a promotion from an influencer and are unsure if your traffic is legitimate, you'll be able to tell based on conversions or lack thereof.

Chapter Summary

- There is a place for both high ticket and low ticket affiliate products in your marketing strategy.
- Be careful when promoting high ticket items since they have a larger impact on the well-being of your audience.
- Although it is more efficient to promote exclusively high ticket products, it is often not in your audience's best interest. Be ethical and promote only the absolute best high ticket offers.

Passive Income Is a Lie

The term "passive income" is priceless for people like me who create content in the make money online space. Why? Because it is one of the sexiest concepts you can imagine. The idea of sitting on a beach sipping margaritas while your phone chirps with alerts of incoming payments is about as good as it gets. The problem is that the concept is over-romanticized and works better in sales copy selling internet business courses than it does in practice.

While it is absolutely possible to collect payments while you sit on the beach drinking margaritas (it's a basic characteristic of affiliate marketing), the money is earned up front. I like to call this *pastive* income. The payouts you make on your beach vacation were earned from the hard work you did in the past—the hard work that didn't result in immediate income.

Furthermore, no passive income is built to last forever. We've discussed the need to regularly update your old content, and I've shown you how we use the skyscraper approach to beat out competitors. If something is making money, your competitors are going to slowly find a way to take some of it.

Deferred Income

Automation and Income Correlation

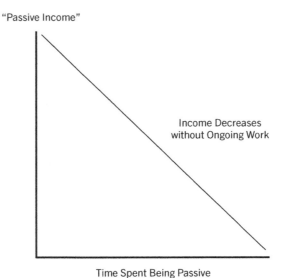

If you're running a paid ad campaign and set it on autopilot, your competitors will eventually emulate your ads and optimize them to beat you. If you grew a large following and stop creating content for them, someone else will come and steal the attention. If you rank in search engines, someone else will skyscrape your article and work to bump you from your top spot.

If you fall too deep into the "passive" mindset, you will almost always see diminishing returns.

There's no shortage of software that can help you automate a great deal of your marketing efforts. You don't need most of them early on. But as you scale, you'll want them since many will have a tremendous impact on your productivity and profitability.

However, just because something can be automated doesn't mean that it should be automated. Automating too much can make you seem robotic and impersonal. That isn't a good recipe for making affiliate sales.

An example of a great automation is sending new email subscribers a welcome email series. One of the biggest mistakes I see email marketers make is that they collect emails but don't contact the subscriber right away. Whenever someone opts-in to your list, you should send them an email welcoming them.

If you're delivering a lead magnet, I highly recommend that you do not allow the subscriber to download it without opening your welcome email. Instead of an instant download or thank you page with a download button, tell subscribers that their lead magnet is in their inbox.

Next, think of the things you want all subscribers to know and do. Your sequence allows you to introduce yourself to the subscriber, provide them with value (which helps increase conversions later), or encourage them to take some other desired action. Other actions could be following you on other social media platforms or buying a low ticket item (this is great for qualifying buyers and offsetting any ad costs). All good email service providers offer some form of email sequence functionality.

Chapter Summary

- Passive income is really just deferred income from hard work put in earlier.
- Falling into autopilot mode too often and for too long will cause you to see diminishing returns.
- Automation is great, but you need to be careful of how much and how often you use it.

Data Lies

Affiliate networks provide us with tons of awesome insights about products. You can see EPC (earnings per click), average refund rate, LTV (lifetime value), and more. However, it is a big mistake to take this information as gospel truth. There is more behind these numbers. Things like:

- Who is promoting them? 90% of the sales could be coming from one dominant affiliate who has extreme authority and trust in a space. If you aren't that authority, your conversions will be lower.
- Who are they selling to? These numbers are going to be reflective of all traffic, but most of the traffic will have been well targeted. So if you think, "I can just run broad ads to this and I'll make that EPC," you will likely end up with a nasty surprise.
- How were they promoted? I have had conversion rates that were four times the average of a product, but there was more to the story. Sometimes I added bonuses or promoted them only to people in a very select segment. I skewed the numbers on that affiliate at least in the short term (sorry everyone).

Don't ignore the data, it's awesome to have, but consider what it really means.

Chapter Summary

- Data is critically important but it can be harmful if you don't understand how to properly analyze it.
- Data for conversion rates is an average of cold, warm, and hot traffic. It also factors in wildly successful affiliate marketers who may be extreme outliers. Don't assume that these rates apply to all traffic types.
- Always err on the side of underestimating the accuracy of data until you've tested for yourself.

Diversify

No matter how much you're sold on a specific affiliate program or product, never let yourself rely on it too much. Although it's great to have your cornerstone products, as we've discussed, you run the risk of losing everything overnight if you focus exclusively on one offer.

- The commission structure could change.
- The company might go out of business.
- The company might sell to new owners who don't want to maintain the affiliate program.
- You could be removed for accidentally violating terms of service.

The list of risks is long enough that putting all of your efforts into just one product is reckless. Remember, you're an affiliate marketer, and one of your great advantages is that you don't need to rely entirely on the success of one particular product.

Likewise, you shouldn't rely entirely on one medium or strategy. As we've discussed, focus on continually growing your owned traffic and never let yourself be tied to any one platform, product, or strategy that could disappear overnight. Diversify, pivot, and thrive.

Chapter Summary

- Relying too much on one affiliate, medium, or tactic is a recipe for disaster.
- Diversify your product offerings and where and how you drive traffic to ensure your business doesn't get wiped out overnight.

Lead Magnet Anatomy

Now that you understand the importance of continually growing your owned traffic, let's talk about how to create enticing lead magnets. A great lead magnet should meet the following six criteria.

Lead Magnets

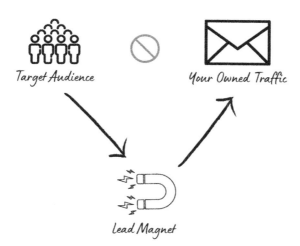

Target Audience

Your Owned Traffic

Lead Magnet

Lead Magnet Rule 1. Provide Immediate Gratification

Your lead magnet needs to be something irresistible and immediately applicable. Someone is much more likely to download your lead magnet if they can use it in the near future. If it's not something they need right now, they likely won't hand over their email address. Your lead magnet can't be vague. It should be extremely targeted to your readers and their current needs.

I have made the mistake many times of associating total value with total opt-ins. The truth is that readers care more about solving their immediate problems than they care about amassing even more information on topics that aren't yet on their mind.

So if your niche is bodybuilding, instead of creating a lead magnet like "Ultimate Guide to Building Muscle," consider something much more simple like "My Simple Cure for Muscle Soreness." The latter is less overwhelming and solves one specific problem (muscle soreness) that relates to your topic of interest. I can almost guarantee that all things being equal, the shorter, targeted lead magnet will outperform the massive "ultimate guide" magnet.

The best lead magnets are downloadable and can be opened by the subscriber quickly and easily. Offering lead magnets that require massive commitments of time (think of something like a "40 week training course") doesn't attract subscribers like magnets that provide the content immediately.

Lead Magnet Rule 2. Attract Your Dream Customer

Many marketers make the mistake of creating freebies that don't define their user base. I've seen people do things like, "Enter to win a free iPad!" The problem with this is that everyone likes free iPads! If someone joins your list because they want an iPad, they aren't likely to be good customers in the future.

Your lead magnet should relate directly to what you are offering your subscribers in the future. Do you plan on promoting a product relating to weight loss? If so, your lead magnet should be related to weight loss!

Lead magnets help you skim the ideal customers from the masses and segment them in a way that allows you to sell to them more easily in the future without being salesy or annoying. If they have already expressed interest in something, you promoting something related to that interest in the future is perfectly natural and welcomed.

Lead Magnet Rule 3. Have Real Value

The lead magnet is a great chance for you to create rapport with your audience. Think of it this way: if your lead magnet provides huge value, the subscriber will ask themselves, "If this is the FREE stuff, what do I get if I buy something?!?" Everything you promote in the future will sell better when you've already built trust and given value freely.

Lead Magnet Rule 4. Demonstrates Your Expertise in Your Field

The free content shouldn't be something you just whip together without any effort. This is your chance to showcase your expertise and impress your new subscribers. Lots of lead magnets end up damaging the reputation of the person or company giving them away because they were put together with little thought or effort.

Now some lead magnets won't check off all four of these rules, and that is okay. But the further you deviate from these guidelines, the lower your conversion rates will become, and you will get subscribers of lesser value.

So where do you start? I have good news, if you already have created content, you likely don't have to start from scratch. Some of the best lead magnets are just repurposed content from blog posts, videos, podcasts, webinars, etc.

Are you worried that people will feel cheated since the information is freely available online? They won't care. No one cares where it came from; it's about value. Just make sure that your magnet provides tons of value. If you don't want to send emails for content that could be found elsewhere, you can always remove the original content after you have made your lead magnet.

A great piece of content can often lead to more revenue in the long run if you use it as a lead magnet as opposed to making it freely available anyway. Just be sure that you don't leave your site barren of the content that makes people visit it in the first place.

Never remove a piece of content that is driving a lot of organic traffic on its own. I'm sure that if you've created a lot of content there is something that is vastly underrated that would serve better as a lead magnet than a stale post or video.

When it comes to creating lead magnets, start with the end in mind. Ask yourself the following questions:

1. What is it you're hoping to sell these subscribers in the future?

Even if you don't have an exact product in mind, you should have a general idea of how you're going to monetize your list in the future. Remember, creating and distributing free content costs you time, energy, and money, so you should have an end in mind for how you'll justify these expenses and then some.

2. What lead magnets could you make to target people who will buy this product in the future?

Let's say that you are hoping to sell something to weight lifters. What sort of lead magnet will work to attract and segment people who will be interested in products in the weight lifting niche? How about a free report showing how to gain an inch on your biceps in three weeks? How about a recipe for the perfect post-workout meal for muscle growth? Both of these ideas will help attract people who are most likely to spend money with you later on in the weight lifting niche.

Here are some ideas for simple lead magnets.

1. Audio File (audiobooks or lessons)
2. Calculator
3. Case Studies
4. Catalog
5. Cheat Sheet
6. Checklist
7. Coupon
8. Desktop Wallpaper
9. Early Bird Access
10. Ebook
11. Email Course
12. Event Tickets
13. Facebook Group Access
14. Free Book and Shipping
15. Free Chapter
16. Free Coaching/Consultation
17. Free Quote
18. Free Shipping
19. Free Trial
20. Gated Content
21. Generator
22. Giveaway
23. Guide
24. Infographic
25. Membership Area
26. Mixed Map
27. Newsletter
28. Plan
29. Predictions
30. Quiz
31. Recipe
32. Replays
33. Resources/Tools List
34. Roundup
35. Script
36. Slack Group
37. Slideshow
38. State of the Industry
39. Summary
40. Survey
41. Swipe File
42. Template
43. Transcript
44. Tutorial
45. Vault/Library
46. Video File
47. Waiting List
48. WebApp
49. Webinar
50. Worksheet/Workbook

Chapter Summary

- Lead magnets are a critical tool for building our owned traffic.
- Great lead magnets should provide immediate

gratification, attract your dream customer, have real value, and demonstrate your expertise in your niche.

- Make it easy for visitors to opt-in to your list and quickly receive their lead magnet. Reduce friction by asking for as little information as you feel is necessary. Typically, name and email are more than plenty.
- Be sure to download the lead magnet checklist at https://evergreenaffiliatemarketing.com/downloads.

Don't Go Revenue Blind

"We're losing money on every sale, but we'll make up for it in volume."

—Old Business Joke

My first exposure to affiliate marketing was from Russian You-Tuber. I've tried to find his channel again just to see how crazy what he teaches looks in hindsight, but it appears he's completely disappeared. The average career lifetime of affiliate marketing gurus is shorter than Chinese leftovers by the way. This was probably for the best.

I remember how he drove to the bank, withdrew a bunch of money, dumped it all on his bed, and proceeded to roll around in it. In a niche that is notoriously cheesy, this took the (cheese) cake. If I wasn't young and inexperienced, I would have just watched it as the comedy that it was rather than an actual educational piece.

Strangely, I do owe him a debt of gratitude since his videos were an eye-opening moment for me. His method was simple. Buy ads for affiliate products that looked promising and earn more on each click than it cost. Unbelievably simple on paper, and extremely exciting for me. I tried it out and managed to squeak out a few sales for a few products that I didn't vet.

My total sales was $900. I told everyone about it. This was a game-changing amount of money for me at the time. I felt so excited to share my results with everyone. That is, until the inevitable question came: "How much of it was profit?" Whoops . . . my profits were actually –$100. I was losing money, but the rush of sales had me excited.

Revenue Blindness

$25,000 in commissions!

$24,970 in ad costs
$30 profit
30 hours spent
$1 per hour

This is the same logic that you experience if you've ever played a slot machine at a casino. You pull the lever and all hell breaks loose. Dings, rings, and flashing lights go crazy and you feel like you're about to leave with a huge payout.

$4!!!! Yes! But wait . . . it was a $5 pull . . .

This concept seems so obvious and almost insulting to mention, but time and time again I've seen affiliate marketers "revenue" their way straight into debt and failure. I've seen many marketers spend small fortunes on paid ads to win contests like cars and trips to the Bahamas only to later find out that the ad cost greatly exceeded the affiliate earnings and the value of the prizes.

Focus on one thing: profits. The only thing to take out of gross sales is data. If it costs you $20 to make a $15 sale, you don't celebrate the $15. You celebrate that you now know that if you can get your ad costs down below $15, you can be profitable. You have a base to build toward success, but you're not there yet. Focus on profits, and everything else is just data for decision fuel.

Chapter Summary

- Although high revenue can be exciting, it means nothing if there isn't true net profit behind it.
- Always be aware of your costs and time. Don't allow yourself to give too much weight to revenue. It is an incomplete metric that can cause you to lose money if you aren't careful.

The Email Tags You Should Use

So without further ado, here are ten of my favorite tagging strategies.

1. Tag Subscribers Based on Interest
Example: 🙄 Interest: Productivity
Reason: Send the right emails to the right subscribers at the right time.

This is the foundation of segmentation. Your interest tags can be narrow and broad, but you should always have them for every single interest your brand targets. I typically create narrow interest tags and then organize those interests into broader segments.

In my email marketing software, I make sure that every lead magnet or source of subscribers has a rule set up that auto-applies a tag. I get even more granular and break up the forms into more narrow tags for hyper-targeted broadcasting and segmentation.

2. Tag Abandoned Carts (If You Have Your Own Product)
Example: 🛒 💸 Abandoned Cart: My Really Cool Software
Reason: Close low-hanging fruit sales.
Don't be shocked when someone leaves a sale hanging at the checkout. You might as well get used to it because the average shopping cart abandonment rate is estimated to be around a staggering 69.8%. There are multiple reasons why someone aban-

doned a purchase, and it isn't always because they don't actually want the item anymore.

- They might have been called away by something.
- They might not have had their credit card handy.
- They might have needed to wait for payday.
- They might have wanted to compare a few alternatives first.
- They might have been on a mobile device (85.6% abandoned cart rate averages) and wanted to wait until they got to desktop.

The list goes on and on. The long and short of it is that you need to continue to sell to these potential buyers with at the very least a polite reminder email.

Abandoned cart subscribers are the epitome of hot traffic, and your conversion rates on your abandoned cart emails should be some of your highest. However, if you aren't tagging these folks, you aren't going to be contacting them!

Note: In order for the abandoned cart functionality to work, you need to have a two-step sales page in place. If they don't submit their email address, you won't have it (duh). I highly recommend that you consider changing all of your sales funnels to two-step order style for this reason.

Abandoned carts are estimated to cost companies $18 billion dollars annually. Minimize the amount of that lost revenue with great tagging and follow up and your bank account will thank you.

Oh, and don't forget to create a removal rule that takes off the abandoned cart tag once someone has purchased.

3. Tag Refunds (If You Have Your Own Product)
Example: 💔 Refunded: My Really Cool Software

Reason 1: So you DON'T sell them the same product.
Reason 2: So you can get feedback and reduce future refunds.
Reason 3: So you can sell an alternative.
Reason 4: So you can flag customers who habitually abuse refunds.

Another important yet often overlooked segmentation method is tagging people who refund your products. Just like with abandoned carts, this doesn't have to be the end of your relationship with a subscriber. You just need to know how to cater to them better. Triggering follow-up automations to refunded customers can be very helpful in understanding how to improve your product or, even better, draw them back to another purchase.

Example Refund Automation Email

Subject: Regarding your refund...
Hey [First Name],

We're sorry to see that [product refunded] didn't meet your expectations.

Your feedback is very important to us and we'd like to know what we could have done differently to better serve your needs.

If you have the time, we'd love for you to take this three-question survey [link to survey] and tell us about your experience.

Upon completion, there is a discount code for 20% off any future purchase with us.

Thank you!

[Signature]

Sending the email above via an automation would allow us to do two things.

1. Get feedback so we can improve
2. Offer a coupon code to encourage the customer to come back.

Be careful with the coupon offer. The last thing you want is word getting out that everyone who refunds can get 20% off! Every business is different, and this is just a broad example, but there is something that can be done with refund-triggered automations for every type of business.

4. Tag Community Members

Example: 🌐 Member: FBA Today Facebook Group
Reason: Increase your exposure without pushing social media channels to existing followers or members.

One of the goals of your email marketing should be to get subscribers to follow you on other mediums. The more exposure you have to someone, the better. It doesn't matter how you connect with your followers, just that you connect with them. This means we need to work to get them on the medium that they like and use the most.

If you have a way of tagging someone who is already in a community, that makes it much easier to filter them out of broadcasts that push subscribers to join it later on. For example, I have a large Facebook group called FBA Today. To join it, you have to provide an email address (this is secretly one of my most effective methods of list building by the way).

This means that I have a large segment of people on my email list that I know are already in the group. I tag them so that I can try to get other subscribers to join the group without bothering existing members with unnecessary emails.

Once someone clicks one of the links, you should tag them as a follower (this part isn't perfect, unfortunately, since many who click won't follow through and actually subscribe or follow). You can then occasionally run campaigns aimed at getting those who didn't click to come and follow you.

5. Tag People with the Lead Magnet They Downloaded

Example: Lead Magnet: Evening Reflections
Reason 1: Give them other unique freebies as value adds to build your relationship further.
Reason 2: Enhanced segmentation.

One of the things that I love to do is send my new subscribers as much free value as possible. Typically, these are things that I also use as lead magnets elsewhere. I have a lot of different freebies I give, and it's not possible for a subscriber to subscribe to all of them, so I use them as bonuses in my email follow ups.

For example, if I know that a subscriber joined this list by downloading Lead Magnet A, I can give them Lead Magnet B as a value add in a follow-up email and vice versa. If you want to learn more about this concept of feeding your new subscribers with value right out of the gate, check out the book The Invisible Selling Machine by Ryan Deiss.

6. Tag Competitors

Example: Other: Competitors
Reason: So they can't spy on you.

This one really isn't that important, and it's not like you can really keep someone from getting your emails if they really want to. But why not at least try a little if it gives you an edge?

I always recommend that people spy on the emails of their competitors to see what strategies may be working for them. If they compete directly with you though, they'd be wise to make it harder for you to see their content.

7. Tag Buyers (If You Have Your Own Product)

Example: 💰 Bought: My Really Cool Software
Reason 1: Avoid annoying them by promoting the same product they've already purchased.
Reason 2: Follow up and get feedback or reviews.
Reason 3: Reduce refunds by adding support follow-up automations.
Reason 4: Promote complementary products effectively.

If you sell a product, always tag your subscribers once they've purchased. This is much more important than many people realize. Have you ever received an email trying desperately to sell you something that you already bought? It's extremely annoying. It makes you feel like the brand doesn't really care that much about you.

Past buyers are your best future customers. Here are some important stats you should be aware of:

- Repeat customers refer 50% more people than one-time buyers.
- Repeat buyers spend 300% more on average than new buyers.
- It costs five times more to acquire a new customer than to keep an existing one.

This is the LAST segment of subscribers you want to ignore. We want to turn one-time buyers into repeat buyers ASAP. Even worse than the mild annoyance of receiving ads for something you already purchased, have you ever received an email with a special discount offer on something you paid full price for? That is a nightmare for email marketers.

"Hey, I paid $149 last year, I see you're doing a $50 off deal . . . Can you honor that and refund me the $50?"

I used to get this type of email quite often when I wasn't properly tagging buyers.

You should be able to run promotions from time to time, but there's no need to rub it into the faces of people who already paid regular price. And I'm sorry, you can't go and refund everyone the difference, that's not in the spirit of promotions and would make them entirely pointless.

8. Create Temporary Tags with Link Triggers

Example: 🚫 Don't Contact: Book Promotion

Reason 1: Know who you should or shouldn't contact regarding specific offers or topics.

Reason 2: Protect relationships with subscribers.

Reason 3: Respect your subscriber's inbox.

Reason 4: Know who your hottest buyers are so you can send them additional relevant offers.

Most other email marketing software allows you to assign tags with something called "link triggers." These help you add information to subscribers whenever they click a certain link. For instance, if someone clicks a link to a blog post about money management, you could set a trigger that adds a tag to them titled "Interested in money management."

Another great temporary tag I use is a "Don't contact me regarding" tag. These are tags that allow subscribers to tell me they don't want to hear any more about a specific offer or topic without completely unsubscribing from my list.

Again, this is very important because to really close sales, you'll need to send more than one email. If I'm doing a large-scale promotion, I always ensure to include this link trigger at the bottom of each email.

For future broadcasts regarding that offer, I'll make sure to create a rule that excludes everyone on this specific tag. These tags can (and should) be deleted once you've completed a promotion and no longer need them.

9. Tag Subscribers for Re-Engagement
Example: ☠ DELETE ☠
Reason: Remove inactive subscribers to protect your email reputation with major email service providers.

Regularly running re-engagement campaigns to cold subscribers will help your list tremendously. It's important that you delete inactive subscribers from your email list regularly. It might sound counterintuitive, but deleting cold subscribers will actually lead to better results in the long run since it will improve the overall deliverability of your broadcasts.

Large providers like Gmail and Outlook take note of whether or not people are opening your emails. If you have a large amount of subscribers who aren't opening, the providers may start sending your emails to the junk or promotions folders for every subscriber, even the ones who actually engage with them.

One of the great things about ConvertKit is that you can add this automation and it will automatically create the tags and framework for you. You'll just want to edit the emails that are sent out in the sequence.

10. Tag Your Affiliates (If You Have Your Own Product)
Example: 🤝 Affiliate: Amazon Products
Reason: Boost overall sales by staying in touch with your affiliates.

Every great affiliate manager understands that you need to regu-larly engage with your affiliates to get them to really promote. Tag your affiliates and keep in touch with them regularly. You can also get even deeper with it and add automations that trigger emails when certain rules are met. When something like "hasn't made a sale in X# days" is triggered, you can send an automated email that reminds the affiliate of the offer and helps encourage them to promote.

What's Next?

Congratulations! If you've made it this far, you've just exposed yourself to the most important principles and tactics of affiliate marketing. You can go forth with the confidence of knowing that there aren't any real "secrets" that others know that you don't. You have everything that you need and understand how to find answers to the new tactics that come and go over time.

Assembly Required

"Knowledge without action is meaningless."

—Abu Bakr

I won't insult your intelligence by reminding you that nothing you just read matters without consistent, focused action. I do, however, want to leave you with some things to consider.

You will forget most of what you just read. Don't believe me? Try to write down the topic of every chapter of this book on a piece of paper and see how many you can recall. This is also immediately after you just spent hours reading. This isn't your fault at all. Even the smartest people in the world recall only a fraction of what they've read.

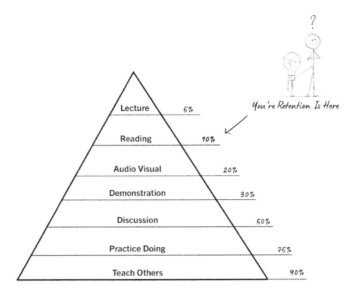

Even if you are one of the few people on the planet who can recall every single concept in this book, not everything will be applicable right now. By the time you reach a point in your career that something becomes relevant, it's even less likely that you recall what I taught you.

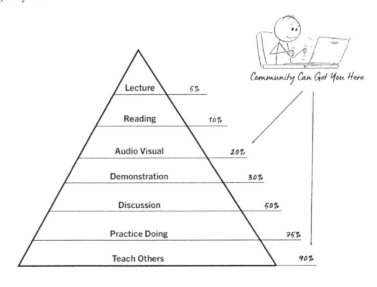

For this reason, I recommend that you keep your copy of *Evergreen Affiliate Marketing* close by so you can refer to it when the time comes. Also, follow me and join my private Facebook community for everyone who purchased the *Evergreen Affiliate Marketing* book. Again, it is completely free for anyone who reads this book, and it will dramatically improve your chances of staying motivated and achieving real success.

https://facebook.com/groups/eambook

Also, don't forget to go grab your free resources and downloads at https://evergreenaffiliatemarketing.com/downloads.

How to Get in Touch with Me

Email me at nate@entreresource.com with anything at all. I welcome any and all messages from my readers. Tell me what you liked, what you didn't like, or what you want to know more about. If you email me, you might not get an instant response, but I guarantee you will get one and it will be from me personally.

Thank you once again for trusting me with your time and energy. I am truly grateful, and I wish you the best of luck in your future success.

My success is tied to your success. Now, go out and make us both successful.

Sincerely,

Nate McCallister

Terms and Definitions

A/B Testing – A testing process in which two or more versions of a variable (web page, page element, etc.) are shown to different segments of website visitors at the same time to identify which version makes the maximum impact. Also known as "split testing."

Advertiser – Another term for the affiliate marketer. "Advertiser" is commonly used in affiliate networks.

Affiliate Link – A unique URL that associates conversions to an affiliate. Clicks and conversions can be tracked easily. Most quality affiliate management software also offers customization options so that efforts can be better analyzed and optimized. See "custom tracking URL."

Affiliate Network – A third party that connects merchants to advertisers. Affiliates can find products to promote and vendors can find affiliates to promote their offers for them.

Associate – Another term for "affiliate" or "advertiser."

Banner Ad – Also referred to as a "display ad," these are graphic ads that advertise a merchant that an affiliate puts on their own websites or buys on third-party websites.

Churn Rate – The percentage of users on a recurring payment plan who cancel each month.

277

Click Attribution – The system that dictates which affiliate click receives credit for the sale. The main attribution models are first click and last click. With first click attribution, the affiliate who caused the consumer to click on the affiliate link first will receive credit for the sale regardless of whether the customer clicks on other advertisers' links later. In contrast, last click attribution credits the sale to the affiliate who sent the last click immediately preceding the sale.

Commission – The payout from a successful affiliate referral. These can be recurring or one-time payments. Not all commissions are paid the same way. Some commissions are paid immediately while others are held until after a refund period has passed.

Cookie – A small file stored on the user's computer that is used to identify the site's visitors. In affiliate marketing, cookies are used to track affiliate referrals.

Cookie Duration – How long a cookie will be active. If a cookie has a duration of thirty days, the affiliate will be attributed credit for the sale if the buyer makes the purchase before thirty days passes.

CPA – Can stand for "cost per action" or "cost per acquisition." This is an affiliate payment model in which affiliates are paid for driving specific actions. They may or may not be actual sales. Some vendors will pay for things such as leads or free trials, regardless of any traditional purchases.

CPC – Stands for "cost per click" and typically refers to the amount an advertiser pays for a visit to their landing pages when using any form of paid advertising platform.

CTR – Stands for "click through rate." This is the number of total clicks divided by total impressions. If you send an email and 100 people open it and see a link and 5 people click on it, your CTR is 5%.

CR – Stands for "conversion rate." This is the percentage of visitors who complete a desired action divided by total clicks. The formula is: Conversions / Clicks = Conversion Rate.

Custom Tracking URL – An affiliate link that has code attached to it that helps identify it more clearly. For example, youraffiliate-product.com/affiliateID/email. The "email" appended at the end of that affiliate link example can help you see which clicks are coming from emails (assuming you share this link only in emails).

EPC – Stands for "earnings per click." This is the average amount of revenue driven by a click. The formula is: Earnings / Number of Unique Clicks = EPC.

Guerilla Marketing – Low-cost marketing efforts that leverage creativity and uniqueness to get attention and drive traffic. This sort of marketing is more subtle than in-your-face paid promotions. Guerrilla marketing can be risky because it may draw backlash and can come off as cheesy or tacky if done carelessly. The examples are endless, but some common methods include having your company's stickers placed where your target customers already are or going, "ethically and legally hijacking" media attention such as the news to get your product incidental attention.

Impressions – In marketing, impressions are views of your content or offer. Many advertisers pay for impressions. Affiliate marketers can get paid for sending impressions for other companies through programs like display ad networks, or they can buy them to get views on their own content or offers.

Lead Magnet – Something of value given in exchange for personal information, usually an email address.

LTV – Abbreviation for "lifetime value," which refers to the average value of a customer over their lifetime as a customer.

Native Advertising – The use of paid ads that match the look and feel of the media format in which they appear.

Pixel – A snippet of code that allows the tracking of a visitor on a website for retargeting once they leave the page.

PPC – Stands for "pay per click." This is a type of advertising where the advertiser pays for each click that is sent to their desired landing page.

Search Engine – A program that searches for and identifies items in a database that correspond to keywords or characters specified by the user; especially used for finding particular sites online. Search engines can be video, audio, or text based. Google and YouTube are the two largest search engines at the time of this writing, but there are many others.

SEM – Stands for "search engine marketing." This includes SEO, but it also includes any other sort of marketing that involves search engines such as paid ads.

SEO – Stands for "search engine optimization." This is the practice of structuring content to rank organically on search engines. There are many different search engines, and what is considered as "optimized" for each of them can vary. This is an appealing method due to its conceived low costs, but the majority of the most successful marketers invest a great amount of time and money into making it work. Bloggers and Vloggers typically focus on SEO.

Made in the USA
Coppell, TX
11 August 2021